The Elements of
of
UML™ Style

The Elements
of
UML™ *Style*

Scott W. Ambler
Ronin International, Inc.

CAMBRIDGE
UNIVERSITY PRESS

PUBLISHED BY THE PRESS SYNDICATE OF THE
UNIVERSITY OF CAMBRIDGE
The Pitt Building, Trumpington Street, Cambridge, United Kingdom

CAMBRIDGE UNIVERSITY PRESS
The Edinburgh Building, Cambridge CB2 2RU, UK
40 West 20th Street, New York, NY 10011-4211, USA
477 Williamstown Road, Port Melbourne, VIC 3166, Australia
Ruiz de Alarcón 13, 28014 Madrid, Spain
Dock House, The Waterfront, Cape Town 8001, South Africa

http://www.cambridge.org

© Cambridge University Press 2003

First published 2003

Printed in the United States of America

Typefaces Adobe Garamond 10.5/12 pt. and ITC Avant Garde
System LATEX 2_ε [TB]

A catalog record for this book is available from the British Library.

Library of Congress Cataloging in Publication Data available

ISBN 0 521 52547 0 paperback

To Sensei Rick Willemsen and Sempai Rick Micucci

Thanks for everything that you have taught me
and continue to teach me.

Contents

Preface

Models are used by professional developers to communicate their work to project stakeholders and to other developers. The Unified Modeling Language (UML) has been an important part of the software development landscape since its introduction in 1997. We've seen the UML evolve over the years, and it is now into its 2.x series of releases. Modeling style, however, has remained constant, and will continue to do so. By understanding and following these common modeling style guidelines, you can improve the effectiveness of your models.

Purpose

This book describes a collection of standards, conventions, and guidelines for creating effective UML diagrams. They are based on sound, proven software engineering principles that will lead to diagrams that are easier to understand and work with.

These simple, concise guidelines, if applied consistently, will be an important first step in increasing your productivity as a modeler.

Features

This guide attempts to emulate Strunk and White's (1979) seminal text, *The Elements of Style*, which lists a set of rules describing the proper application of grammatical and compositional forms in common use within the written English language.

Using a similar style of presentation, this book defines a set of rules for developing high-quality UML diagrams. In doing so, this guide

- employs existing standards defined by the Object Management Group (OMG) whenever possible,
- provides a justification for each rule, and
- presents standards based on real-world experience and proven software-engineering principles.

Audience

This guide targets professional software developers who are interested in

- creating effective UML diagrams,
- increasing their productivity, and
- working as productive members of an object-oriented development team.

Assumptions

In this book I make several assumptions:

- You understand the basics of the UML and modeling. If not, then I suggest *UML Distilled* (Fowler and Scott 1999) if you are looking for a brief overview of the UML or *The Object Primer 2/e* (Ambler 2001) for a more comprehensive discussion. *UML Distilled* is a great book but is limited to the UML; *The Object Primer 2/e*, on the other hand, goes beyond the UML where needed, for example, to include user interface, Java, and database development issues.

- You are looking for style guidelines, not design guidelines. If not, then I suggest the book *Object-Oriented Design Heuristics* (Riel 1996).
- Your focus is on business application development. Although these guidelines also apply to real-time development, all of the examples are business application oriented, simplifications of actual systems that I have built in the past.
- You belong to a Western culture. Many of the layout guidelines are based on the Western approach to reading—left to right and top down. People in other cultures will need to modify these guidelines as appropriate.

Acknowledgments

The following people have provided valuable input into the development and improvement of this text: James Bielak, Lauren Cowles, Caitlin Doggart, Scott Fleming, Alvery Grazebrook, Kirk W. Knoernschild, Hubert Matthews, Les Munday, Sabine Noack, Paul Oldfield, Leo Tohill, and Robert White.

1.

Introduction

One of Agile Modeling's (AM) (Ambler 2002) practices is *Apply Modeling Standards,* the modeling version of eXtreme Programming (XP)'s *Coding Standards* (Beck 2000). Developers should agree to and follow a common set of standards and guidelines on a software project, and some of those guidelines should apply to modeling. Models depicted with a common notation and that follow effective style guidelines are easier to understand and to maintain. These models will improve communication internally within your team and externally to your partners and customers, thereby reducing the opportunities for costly misunderstandings. Modeling guidelines will also save you time by limiting the number of stylistic choices you face, allowing you to focus on your actual job, which is to develop software.

> A lot of the communication value in a UML diagram
> is still due to the layout skill of the modeler.
> —Paul Evitts, *A UML Pattern Language*

When adopting modeling standards and guidelines within your organization, your first goal is to settle on a common notation. The Unified Modeling Language (UML) (Object Management Group 2001, U2 Partners 2002) is a good start because it defines the notation and semantics for common object-oriented models. Some projects will require more types of models than the UML describes, as I show in *The Object Primer 2/e* (Ambler 2001), but the UML will form the core of any modern modeling effort.

Your second step is to identify modeling style guidelines to help you create consistent and clean-looking diagrams. What is the difference between a standard and a style guideline? For source code, a standard would, for example, involve naming the attributes in the format *attributeName,* whereas a style guideline would involve indenting your code within a control structure by three spaces. For models, a standard would involve using a squared rectangle to model a class on a class diagram, whereas a style would involve placing subclasses on diagrams below their superclass(es). This book describes the style guidelines that are missing from many of the UML-based methodologies that organizations have adopted, guidelines that are critical to your success in the software development game.

The third step is to adopt your modeling standards and guidelines. To do this, you will need to train and mentor your staff in the modeling techniques appropriate to the projects on which they are working. You will also need to train and mentor them in your adopted guidelines, and a good start is to provide them with a copy of this book. I've been amazed at the success of *The Elements of Java Style* (Vermeulen et al. 2000) with respect to this—hundreds of organizations have adopted that book for their internal Java coding standards because they recognized that it was more cost-effective for them to buy a pocketbook for each developer than to develop their own guidelines.

1.1 Organization of This Book

This book is organized in a straightforward manner. Chapter 2 describes general diagramming principles that are applicable to all types of UML diagrams (and many non-UML diagrams for that matter). Chapters 3 through 11 describe techniques pertinent to each type of UML diagram, including package diagrams. Chapter 12 provides an overview of the values, principles, and practices of AM, with a quick reference to this popular methodology. Finally, Chapter 13 lists all of the guidelines presented in this book.

2.

General

Diagramming

Guidelines

The guidelines presented in this chapter are applicable to all types of diagrams. The terms "symbols," "lines," and "labels" are used throughout:

- Symbols represent diagram elements such as class boxes, object boxes, use cases, and actors.
- Lines represent diagram elements such as associations, dependencies, and transitions between states.
- Labels represent diagram elements such as class names, association roles, and constraints.

2.1 Readability Guidelines

1. Avoid Crossing Lines

When two lines cross on a diagram, such as two associations on a UML class diagram, the potential for misreading a diagram exists.

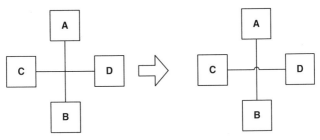

Figure 1. Depiction of crossing lines.

2. Depict Crossing Lines as a Jump

You can't always avoid crossing lines; for example, you cannot fully connect five symbols (try it and see). When you need to have two lines cross, one of them should "hop" over the other as in Figure 1.

3. Avoid Diagonal or Curved Lines

Straight lines, drawn either vertically or horizontally, are easier for your eyes to follow than are diagonal or curved lines. A good approach is to place symbols on diagrams as if they are centered on the grid point of a graph, a built-in feature of many CASE tools. This makes it easier to connect your symbols by only using horizontal and vertical lines. Note how three lines are improved in Figure 2 when this approach is taken. Also note how the line between *A* and *C* has been depicted in "step fashion" as a line with vertical and horizontal segments.

4. Apply Consistently Sized Symbols

The larger a symbol appears, the more important it seems to be. In the first version of the diagram in Figure 2, the *A* symbol is larger than the others, drawing attention to it. If that isn't the effect that you want, then strive to make your symbols of uniform size. Because the size of some symbols is determined by their contents—for example, a class will vary in size based

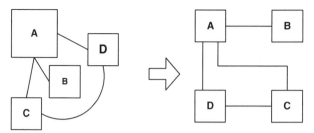

Figure 2. Improving the attractiveness of a diagram.

on its attributes and operations—this rule is not universally applicable.

5. *Arrange Symbols Symmetrically*

Figure 3 presents a UML activity diagram (Chapter 9) depicting a high-level approach to enterprise modeling. Organizing

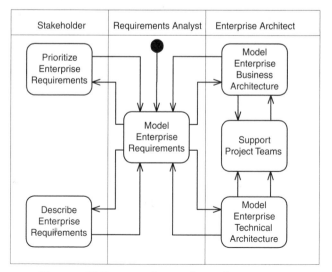

Figure 3. UML activity diagram for a software process.

the symbols and lines in a symmetrical manner makes the diagram easier to understand.

6. *Include White Space in Diagrams*

White space is the empty areas between modeling elements on your diagrams. In the first version of Figure 2 the symbols are crowding each other, whereas in the second version, the symbols are spread out from one another, thus improving the readability of the diagram. Observe that in the second version there is adequate space to add labels to the lines.

7. *Organize Diagrams Left to Right, Top to Bottom*

In Western culture, people read left to right and top to bottom and therefore this is how they will read your diagrams. If there is a starting point for reading the diagram, such as the initial state of a UML state chart diagram or the beginning of the flow of logic on a UML sequence diagram, then place it toward the top-left corner of your diagram and continue appropriately from there.

2.2 Simplicity Guidelines

8. *Show Only What You Have to Show*

Diagrams showing too many details are difficult to read because they are too information dense. One of the practices of Agile Modeling (Chapter 12) is to *Depict Models Simply*, to include only critical information on your diagrams, and to exclude anything extraneous. A simple model that shows the key features that you are trying to depict—perhaps a UML Class diagram depicting the primary responsibilities of classes and the relationships between them—often proves to be sufficient. Yes, you could model all of the scaffolding code that you will need to implement, but what value would that add? Very little.

9. *Prefer Well-Known Notation over Esoteric Notation*

Diagrams that include esoteric notation, instead of just the 20 percent "core notation" that does 80 percent of the job, can be difficult to read. An improvement in UML 2.x over UML 1.x is the explicit definition of that core notation to identify the primary notation that developers need to understand. Of course, what is well known in one organization may not be so well-known in another, and so, you may want to consider supplying people with a brief summary of the notation that you're using.

10. *Reorganize Large Diagrams into Several Smaller Ones*

It is often better to have several diagrams showing various degrees of detail than one complex diagram that shows everything. A good rule of thumb is that a diagram shouldn't have more than 9 symbols on it, based on the $7 +/- 2$ rule (Miller 1957), because there is a limit on the amount of information that someone can deal with at once. "Wallpaper" diagrams, particularly enterprise data models or enterprise object models, may look interesting but they're too information-dense to be effective. When you are reorganizing a large diagram into several smaller ones, you may choose to introduce a high-level package diagram (Chapter 5).

11. *Prefer Single-Page Diagrams*

To reduce complexity, a diagram should be printable on a single sheet of paper to help reduce its scope as well as to prevent wasted time cutting and taping several pages together. Be aware that you will reduce the usability of a diagram if you need to reduce the font too much or crowd the symbols and lines.

12. *Focus on Content First, Appearance Second*

There is always the danger of adding hours onto your CASE tool modeling efforts by rearranging the layout of your

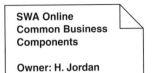

Figure 4. A summary note for a diagram.

symbols and lines to improve the diagram's readability. The best approach is to focus on the content of a diagram at first and only try to get it looking good in a rough sort of way—it doesn't have to be perfect while you're working on it. Once you're satisfied that your diagram is accurate enough, and that you want to keep it, then invest the appropriate time to make it look good. An advantage of this approach is that you don't invest significant effort improving diagrams that you eventually discard.

13. Describe Diagrams with a Note

Ever look at a diagram and not know what it represents? A simple solution is to include a UML Note on each diagram that provides a simple and concise description. This is often referred to as a "legend." In Figure 4 you can see that the name of the system, the purpose of the diagram, and its owner are indicated. It is common also to indicate when the diagram was last updated and the contact information for the owner.

14. Set a Convention for Placement of Diagram Legends

Placing diagram legends in the same place on all of your diagrams increases their usability by making them easy to find. Common spots are one of the corners or the bottom center of a diagram.

15. Apply Consistent, Readable Fonts

Consistent, easy-to-read fonts improve the readability of your diagrams. Good ideas include fonts in the Courier, Arial, and Times families. Bad ideas include small fonts (less than 10 point), large fonts (greater than 18 point), and italics.

2.3 Naming Guidelines

16. Set and Follow Effective Naming Conventions

This is one of the easiest things that you can do to ensure consistency within your models, and hence increase their readability.

17. Apply Common Domain Terminology in Names

Apply consistent and recognizable domain terminology, such as customer and order, whenever possible on your diagrams. This is particularly true for requirements and analysis-oriented diagrams with which your project stakeholders are likely to be working.

18. Apply Language Naming Conventions on Design Diagrams

Design diagrams should reflect implementation issues, including language naming conventions, such as *orderNumber* for an attribute and *sendMessage()* in Java. Requirements and analysis-oriented diagrams should not reflect language issues such as this.

19. Name Common Elements Consistently Across Diagrams

A single modeling element, such as an actor or a class, will appear on several of your diagrams. For example, the same class will appear on several UML class diagrams, several UML sequence diagrams, several UML collaboration diagrams, and several UML activity diagrams. This class should have the same name on each diagram, otherwise your readers will become confused.

2.4 General Guidelines

20. *Indicate Unknowns with a Question Mark*

While you are modeling, you may discover that you do not have complete information. This is particularly true when you are analyzing the domain. You should always try to track down a sufficient answer, but if you cannot do so immediately, then make a good guess and indicate your uncertainty. Figure 5 depicts a common way to do so with its use of question marks.[1] First, there is a note attached to the association between *Professor* and *Seminar* questioning the multiplicity. Second, there is a question mark above the constraint on the *wait listed* association between *Student* and *Seminar*, likely an indication that the modeler isn't sure that it really is a first in, first out (FIFO) list.

21. *Consider Applying Color to Your Diagrams*

Coad, Lefebvre, and DeLuca (1999) provide excellent advice in their book, *Java Modeling in Color with UML,* for improving the understandability of your diagrams by applying color to them, in addition to UML stereotypes. Perhaps color could indicate the implementation language of a class (e.g., blue for Java and red for C++) on a UML Class diagram, the development priority of a use case (e.g., red for phase 1, orange for phase 2, and yellow for future phases) on a UML use case diagram, or the target platform (e.g., blue for an application server, green for a client machine, and pink for a database server) for a software element on a UML deployment diagram.

22. *Apply Color or Different Fonts Sparingly*

Evitts (2000) suggests the use of different fonts, line styles, colors, and shading to emphasize different aspects of your

---

[1] Question marks are not official UML notation.

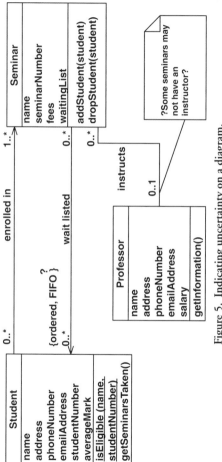

Figure 5. Indicating uncertainty on a diagram.

11

diagrams. The secret is to do so sparingly, otherwise you run the risk of creating noisy/gaudy diagrams. Sometimes less is more.

2.5 Common UML Modeling Elements Guidelines

23. *Left-Justify Text in Notes*

It is common practice to left-justify text in UML notes, as you can see in Figure 4 and Figure 5.

24. *Name Stereotypes in* `<<user interface>>` *and* `<<UI>>` *Format*

It is common UML convention to use lowercase for stereotypes that are spelled out fully, such as `<<include>>` instead of `<<Include>>`, and to use all uppercase for stereotypes that are abbreviations, such as `<<HTTP>>` instead of `<<Http>>`.

25. *Prefer Naming Conventions over Stereotypes*

An effective alternative to applying a stereotype is to apply a naming convention. For example, instead of applying the stereotype `<<getter>>` on an operation, you could simply start all getters with the text *get,* as you can see in Figure 5 with the *getSeminarsTaken()* operation. This simplifies your diagrams and increases the consistency of your source code.

26. *Introduce New Stereotypes Sparingly*

A common mistake made by UML novices is to apply stereotypes to everything, forcing them to introduce a plethora of new stereotypes. The end result is that their diagrams are cluttered with stereotypes. Introduce a new stereotype to clarify an aspect of a model, but don't introduce one simply to "complete" your models.

27. Apply Stereotypes Consistently

You will find that you need to document your common stereotypes, above and beyond those defined by the UML standard, to ensure that they are applied consistently. For example, you need to decide whether you are going to use <<user interface>> or <<UI>> as your preferred stereotype. Both are good choices; choose one and move forward.

28. Prefer Notes over OCL or ASL to Indicate Constraints

Constraints can be modeled on any UML diagram. A constraint is a restriction on the degree of freedom you have in providing a solution. In UML, constraints are modeled either by a UML note using free-form text or with Object Constraint Language (OCL) (Warmer and Kleppe 1999) in UML 1.x and Action Semantic Language (ASL) in UML 2.x.

Figure 5 includes a very simple example of OCL, {*ordered, FIFO*}, code that programmers may understand but few project stakeholders are likely to. When the audience for a diagram includes project stakeholders, you should write a free-form note, perhaps using natural language, for your constraint. Consider OCL or ASL for diagrams whose only audience is developers, but recognize that this is only appropriate if everyone involved understands OCL or ASL.

3.

UML Use Case Diagrams

A UML use case diagram shows the relationships among actors and use cases within a system. They are often used to

- provide an overview of all or part of the usage requirements for a system or organization in the form of an essential model (Constantine and Lockwood 1999; Ambler 2001) or a business model (Rational Corporation 2002),
- communicate the scope of a development project, and
- model your analysis of your usage requirements in the form of a system use case model (Cockburn 2001; Ambler 2001).

A use case model is comprised of one or more use case diagrams and any supporting documentation such as use case specifications and actor definitions. Within most use case models, the use case specifications tend to be the primary artifact, with UML use case diagrams filling a supporting role as the "glue" that keeps your requirements model together. Use case models should be developed from the point of view of your project stakeholders and not from the (often technical) point of view of developers.

3.1 Use Case Guidelines

A use case describes a sequence of actions that provide a measurable value to an actor. A use case is drawn as a horizontal ellipse on a UML use case diagram, as you can see in Figure 6.

29. Begin Use Case Names with a Strong Verb

Good use case names include *Withdraw Funds, Register Student in Seminar,* and *Deliver Shipment* because it is clear what each use case does. Use case names beginning with weak verbs such as "process," "perform," and "do" are often problematic. Such names often result in communication difficulties with your project stakeholders, people who are far more likely to say that they withdraw funds from accounts instead of process withdrawal transactions. These communication difficulties are likely to decrease your ability to understand their requirements. Furthermore, names such as *Process Withdrawal Transaction* or *Perform Student Enrollment Request* often indicate that the use case was written with a technically

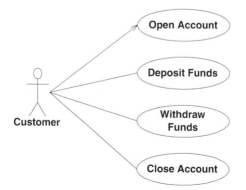

Figure 6. Implying timing considerations between use cases.

oriented view instead of a user-oriented view, and therefore may be at risk of not reflecting the actual needs of your project stakeholders.

30. Name Use Cases Using Domain Terminology

The name of a use case should immediately convey meaning to your project stakeholders. For example, *Convey Package Via Vehicular Transportation* is a generic name for a use case but *Deliver Shipment* reflects common domain terminology and therefore is more understandable.

31. Imply Timing Considerations by Stacking Use Cases

Although use case diagrams should not reflect timing considerations, such as the need to work through use case *A* before proceeding to use case *B*, the fact is that you can increase the readability of your use case diagrams by arranging use cases to imply timing. One such way is to stack them, as you can see in Figure 6, so that the use cases that typically occur first are shown above those that appear later. Note that the order in which these use cases are invoked is only implied; throughout most of the life of a bank account, you can deposit to it or withdraw from it in any order that you like, assuming you conform to the appropriate business rules when doing so.

You can define preconditions in your use cases to describe timing considerations, such as the need for an online shopper to define his or her default address information before being allowed to place an order. You may want to consider drawing an activity diagram representing the overall business process instead of indicating timing considerations on your use case diagrams.

Note that Figure 6 goes against the general guideline *Avoid Diagonal or Curved Lines*—but it's a small diagram, and so, the diagonal lines are still easy to follow from one model element to another.

3.2 Actor Guidelines

An actor is a person, organization, local process (e.g., system clock), or external system that plays a role in one or more interactions with your system (actors are drawn as stick figures).

32. Place Your Primary Actor(s) in the Top-Left Corner of the Diagram

In Western cultures, you start reading in the top-left corner. All things being equal, this is the best location for your primary actors, who are often directly involved with your primary/critical use cases.

For example, you can see in Figure 7 that *Customer* is placed near the top-left corner of the diagram as opposed to the *Customer Support* actor that is placed on the right-hand side. Also notice how the two most-critical use cases, the ones supporting the sale of items on the Web site, are also placed at the top left, and the guideline *Imply Timing Considerations By Stacking Use Cases* has also been applied to order *Search for Items* and *Place Order*.

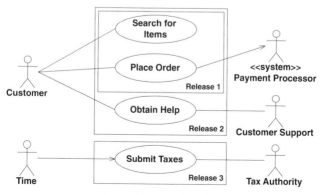

Figure 7. Online shopping.

33. Draw Actors on the Outside Edges of a Use Case Diagram

By definition, actors are outside your scope of control, something that you can communicate by drawing them on the outside edges of a use case diagram, as you can see in Figure 7.

34. Name Actors with Singular, Domain-Relevant Nouns

An actor should have a name that accurately reflects its role within your model. Actor names are usually singular nouns such as *Grade Administrator*, *Customer*, and *Payment Processor*.

35. Associate Each Actor with One or More Use Cases

Every actor is involved with at least one use case, and every use case is involved with at least one actor. Note that there isn't necessarily a one-to-one relationship between actors and use cases. For example, in Figure 7 you can see that *Customer* is involved with several use cases and that the use case *Obtain Help* has two actors interacting with it.

36. Name Actors to Model Roles, Not Job Titles

A common mistake when naming actors is to use the names of job titles that people hold instead of the roles that the people fulfill. This results in actors with names such as *Junior CSR*,[2] *Lead CSR*, and *CSR Manager* instead of *Customer Support* as you can see in Figure 7. A good indication that you are modeling job titles instead of roles is a use case diagram depicting several actors with similar names that have associations to the same use case(s). Modeling roles instead of job titles will simplify your diagrams and will avoid the problem of coupling your use case diagram to the current position hierarchy within your organization: you wouldn't want to have to update your models simply because your human resources department replaced the term *CSR* with *Support Engineer*. However, if you

---

[2] CSR = Customer Service Representative.

are working in a politically charged environment where it is advantageous for you to show certain positions on a use case diagram, feel free to do so at your own discretion.

37. Use <<system>> to Indicate System Actors

In Figure 7, you immediately know that *Payment Processor* is a system and not a person or organization because of the stereotype applied to it. The <<system>> stereotype is applicable to system/concrete use case diagrams that reflect architectural decisions made for your system as opposed to essential use case diagrams (Constantine and Lockwood 1999) or business use case diagrams (Rational Corporation 2002), that are technology independent.

38. Don't Allow Actors to Interact with One Another

The nature of the interaction between two actors will be captured in the text of the use case, not pictorially on your use case diagram.

39. Introduce an Actor Called "Time" to Initiate Scheduled Events

Certain events happen on a regular basis—payroll is fulfilled every two weeks, bills are paid once a month, and staff evaluations are held annually. In Figure 7, you can see that the *Time* actor initiates the *Submit Taxes* use case because it is something that occurs on a periodic basis (typically monthly).

3.3 Relationship Guidelines

There are several types of relationships that may appear on a use case diagram:

- an association between an actor and a use case,
- an association between two use cases,
- a generalization between two actors,
- a generalization between two use cases.

Associations are depicted as lines connecting two modeling elements with an optional open-headed arrowhead on one end of the line, indicating the direction of the initial invocation of the relationship. Generalizations are depicted as a close-headed arrow with the arrow pointing toward the more general modeling element.

40. Indicate an Association Between an Actor and a Use Case if the Actor Appears Within the Use Case Logic

Your use case diagram should be consistent with your use cases. If an actor supplies information, initiates the use case, or receives any information as a result of the use case, then the corresponding use case diagram should depict an association between the two. As you can see in Figure 8, these types of associations are depicted with solid lines. Note that if you are taking an Agile Modeling (AM) approach to development your artifacts don't need to be perfectly in sync with each other—they just need to be good enough.

41. Avoid Arrowheads on Actor-Use Case Relationships

The arrowheads on actor-use case associations indicate who or what invokes the interaction. Indicate an arrowhead only

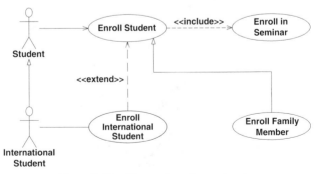

Figure 8. Enrolling students in a university.

when doing so provides significant value, such as when it is important to indicate that an actor is passive regarding its interaction with your system, or when your audience for the model understands the implications of the arrowhead.

In Figure 8, *Student* invokes the *Enroll Student* use case, whereas in Figure 7 the *Place Order* use case initiates the interaction with the *Payment Processor* actor. Although this is perfectly fine, the problem is that many people think that these arrowheads imply information or data flow, such as you would see in a data flow diagram (Gane and Sarson 1979; Ambler 1997), instead of initial invocation. Associations do not represent information; they merely indicate that an actor is somehow involved with a use case. Yes, there is information flowing back and forth between the actor and the use case; for example, students would need to indicate in which seminars they wish to enroll and the system would need to indicate to the student whether or not they have been enrolled.

42. *Apply* <<include>> *When You Know Exactly When to Invoke the Use Case*

In Figure 8 the *Enroll Student* use case includes the use case *Enroll in Seminar*. It is modeled like this because, at a specific point in *Enroll Student,* the logic encapsulated by the included use case is required. In this example, part of the task of enrolling a student in the university is also initially to enroll that student in one or more seminars, something that is done at a specific step in the use case.

The best way to think of an <<include>> association is as the invocation of one use case by another one, just like calling a function or invoking an operation within source code. It is quite common to introduce a use case that encapsulates common logic required by several use cases and to have that use case included by the ones that require it. It is also common for one use case to include another when the logic of the included use case is invoked in a synchronous manner. All <<include>> associations, as well as <<extend>> associations, are modeled as dependencies between use cases and therefore a dashed line is used, as you can see in Figure 8.

43. Apply <<extend>> When a Use Case May Be Invoked Across Several Use Case Steps

In Figure 8, you can see that the *Enroll International Student* use case extends the *Enroll Student* use case. It is modeled this way because the extending use case defines logic that may be required during a given set of steps in the parent use case. In this example, international students are subject to additional scrutiny during the enrollment task, something that will occur sometime after their basic name and address information has been taken but before they are given their student information package—anywhere within a range of use case steps.

An <<extend>> association is a generalization relationship where the extending use case continues the behavior of the base use case by conceptually inserting additional action sequences into the base use case, steps that may work parallel (asynchronously) to the existing use case steps. One way to think of extension is to consider it the use case equivalent of a hardware interrupt—you're not sure when or if the interrupt will occur. It is quite common to introduce an extending use case whenever the logic for an alternate course of action is at a complexity level similar to that of your basic course of action or when you require an alternate course for an alternate course (in this case the extending use case would encapsulate both alternate courses).

44. Apply <<extend>> Associations Sparingly

Many use case modelers avoid the use of <<extend>> associations because they have a tendency to make use case diagrams difficult to understand.

45. Generalize Use Cases When a Single Condition Results in Significantly New Business Logic

In Figure 8, you can see that the *Enroll Family Member* use case inherits from the *Enroll Student* use case. It is modeled this way because the inheriting use case describes similar yet different business logic than the base use case and therefore either the basic course of action or one or more alternate courses of action within the use case are completely rewritten. In this example, you enroll family members of university professors in a similar manner to that for "normal students," the main differences being that several enrollment requirements are reduced or removed completely and the university fees are calculated differently (residence and seminar fees are charged at a reduced rate and all incidental fees are waived).

Inheritance between use cases is not as common as either the use of <<extend>> or <<include>> associations, but it is still possible.

46. *Do Not Apply* <<uses>>, <<includes>>, *or* <<extends>>

All three of these stereotypes were supported by earlier versions of the UML but over time have been replaced—<<uses>> and <<includes>> were both replaced by <<include>>, and <<extends>> was reworked into <<extend>> and generalization. You will likely find these stereotypes applied on old use case diagrams because experienced use case modelers may not yet have transitioned to the newer stereotypes for use case associations.

47. Avoid More Than Two Levels of Use Case Associations

Whenever your use case diagram shows that a use case includes another use case, which includes another use case, which in turn includes yet another use case, it is a very good indication that you are taking a functional decomposition approach to your usage requirements. Functional decomposition is a design activity, and you should avoid reflecting design decisions within your requirements artifacts.

48. Place an Included Use Case to the Right of the Invoking Use Case

It is common convention to draw <<include>> relationships horizontally, with the included use case to the right of the invoking use case, as you can see in Figure 8 with *Enroll Student* and *Enroll in Seminar.*

49. Place an Extending Use Case Below the Parent Use Case

It is common convention to draw <<extend>> relationships vertically, with the extending use case placed lower on your diagram than the base use case, as you can see in Figure 8 with *Enroll International Student* and *Enroll Student.*

50. Apply the "Is Like" Rule to Use Case Generalization

The sentence "the [inheriting use case name] is like the [parent use case name]" should make sense. In Figure 8, it makes sense to say that enrolling a family member is like enrolling a student; therefore, it's a good indication that generalization makes sense. It doesn't make sense to say that enrolling a student is like enrolling in a seminar. The logic for each activity is different—although the two use cases may be related, it isn't by generalization.

51. Place an Inheriting Use Case Below the Base Use Case

It is a common convention to draw generalization relationships vertically, with the inheriting use case placed lower on your diagram than the parent use case, as you can see in Figure 8 with *Enroll Family Member* and *Enroll Student.*

52. *Apply the "Is Like" Rule to Actor Inheritance*

The sentence "the [inheriting actor name] is like the [parent actor name]" should make sense. In Figure 8, it makes sense to say that an international student is like a student; therefore it's a good indication that generalization makes sense. It doesn't make sense in Figure 7 to say that customer support is like a payment processor because the two roles are clearly different.

53. *Place an Inheriting Actor Below the Parent Actor*

It is a common convention to draw generalization relationships vertically, with the inheriting actor placed lower on your diagram than the parent actor, as you can see in Figure 8 with *International Student* and *Student.*

3.4 System Boundary Box Guidelines

The rectangle around the use cases is called the system boundary box and, as the name suggests, it indicates the scope of your system—the use cases inside the rectangle represent the functionality that you intend to implement.

54. *Indicate Release Scope with a System Boundary Box*

In Figure 7, you can see that three system boundary boxes are included, each of which has a label indicating the release to which the various use cases have been assigned. This project team is taking an incremental approach to software development and therefore needs to communicate to their project stakeholders what will be delivered in each release, and they have done so using system boundary boxes.

Notice how the nature of each release is indicated by the placement of each system boundary box. You can see that release 2 includes release 1, whereas release 3 is separate. The team may be trying to indicate that, during release 2, they expect to enhance the functionality initially provided by release 1, whereas they don't expect to do so during release 3. Or perhaps they intend to develop release 3 parallel to release 1 and/or 2. The exact details aren't readily apparent from the diagram. You could add a note, if appropriate, but the diagram would support information contained in another project artifact such as your project plan.

Figure 7 should have included another system boundary box, one encompassing all three releases to specify the exact boundary of the overall system, but it doesn't. I did this in accordance with AM's (Chapter 12) *Depict Models Simply* practice, making the assumption that the readers of the diagram would read between the lines.

55. *Avoid Meaningless System Boundary Boxes*

System boundary boxes are optional—neither Figure 6 nor Figure 8 includes one because it wouldn't add to the communication value of the diagram.

4.

UML Class

Diagrams

UML class diagrams show the classes of the system, their inter-relationships, and the operations and attributes of the classes. They are used to

- explore domain concepts in the form of a domain model,
- analyze requirements in the form of a conceptual/analysis model, and
- depict the detailed design of object-oriented or object-based software.

A class model comprises one or more class diagrams, and the supporting specifications that describe model elements including classes, relationships between classes, and interfaces.

4.1 General Guidelines

Because UML class diagrams are used for a variety of purposes—from understanding your requirements to describing your detailed design—you will need to apply a different style in each circumstance. This section describes style guidelines pertaining to different types of class diagrams.

56. Identify Responsibilities on Domain Class Models

When creating a domain class diagram, often as part of your requirements modeling efforts, focus on identifying responsibilities for classes instead of on specific attributes or operations. For example, the *Invoice* class is responsible for providing its total, but whether it maintains this as an attribute or simply calculates it at request time is a design decision that you'll make later.

There is some disagreement about this guideline because it implies that you should be taking a responsibility-driven approach to development. Craig Larman (2002) suggests a data-driven approach, where you start domain models by identifying only data attributes, resulting in a model that is little different from a logical data model. If you need to create a logical data model, then do so, following AM's practice, *Apply the Right Artifact(s)* (Chapter 12). However, if you want to create a UML class diagram, then you should consider the whole picture and identify responsibilities.

57. Indicate Visibility Only on Design Models

The visibility of an operation or attribute defines the level of access that objects have to it, and the UML supports four types of visibility that are summarized in Table 1. Visibility is an important design issue. On detailed design models, you should always indicate the visibility of attributes and operations, an issue that typically is not pertinent to domain or conceptual

Table 1. Visibility options on UML class diagrams.

Visibility	Symbol	Accessible to
Public	+	All objects within your system
Protected	#	Instances of the implementing class and its subclasses
Private	−	Instances of the implementing class
Package	∼	Instances of classes within the same package

models. Visibility on an analysis or domain model will always be public (+), and so, there is little value in indicating this.

58. Indicate Language-Dependent Visibility with Property Strings

If your implementation language includes non-UML-supported visibilities, such as C++'s implementation visibility, then a property string should be used, as you can see in Figure 9.

59. Indicate Types on Analysis Models Only When the Type Is an Actual Requirement

Sometimes the specific type of an attribute is a requirement. For example, your organization may have a standard definition for customer numbers that requires that they be a nine-digit number. Perhaps existing systems, such as a legacy database or a predefined data feed, constrain some data elements to a specific type or size. If this is the case, you should indicate this information on your domain class model(s).

Analysis

Order
Placement Date Delivery Date Order Number
Calculate Total Calculate Taxes

Design

Order
- deliveryDate: Date - orderNumber: int - placementDate: Date - taxes: Currency - total: Currency
calculateTaxes(Country, State): Currency # calculateTotal(): Currency getTaxEngine() {visibility=implementation}

Figure 9. Analysis and design versions of a class.

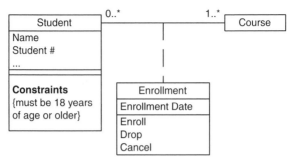

Figure 10. Modeling association classes.

60. Be Consistent with Attribute Names and Types

It would not be consistent for an attribute named *customer-Number* to be a string, although it would make sense for it to be an integer. However, it would be consistent for the name *customerID* to be a string or an integer.

61. Model Association Classes on Analysis Diagrams

Association classes, also called link classes, are used to model associations that have methods and attributes. Figure 10 shows that association classes are depicted as a class attached via a dashed line to an association—the association line, the class, and the dashed line are considered to be one symbol in the UML. Association classes typically are modeled during analysis and then refactored during design (either by hand or automatically by your CASE tool) because mainstream programming languages do not (yet) have native support for this concept.

62. Do Not Name Associations That Have Association Classes

The name of the association class should adequately describe it. Therefore, as you can see in Figure 10, the association does not need an additional adornment indicating its name.

63. Center the Dashed Line of an Association Class

The dashed line connecting the class to the association path should be clearly connected to the path and not to either class or to any adornments of the association so that your meaning is clear. As you can see in Figure 10, the easiest way to accomplish this is to center the dashed line on the association path.

4.2 Class Style Guidelines

A class is effectively a template from which objects are created (instantiated). Classes define attributes, information that is pertinent to their instances, and operations—functionality that the objects support. Classes also realize interfaces (more on this later). Note that you may need to soften some of these naming guidelines to reflect your implementation language or any purchased or adopted software.

64. Use Common Terminology for Class Names

Class names should be based on commonly accepted terminology to make them easier to understand by others. For business classes, this would include names based on domain terminology such as *Customer*, *OrderItem*, and *Shipment* and, for technical classes, names based on technical terminology such as *MessageQueue*, *ErrorLogger*, and *PersistenceBroker*.

65. Prefer Complete Singular Nouns for Class Names

Names such as *Customer* and *PersistenceBroker* are preferable to *Cust* and *PBroker*, respectively, because they are more descriptive and thus easier to understand. Furthermore, it is common practice to name classes as singular nouns such as *Customer* instead of *Customers*. Even if you have a class that does represent several objects, such as an iterator (Gamma et al. 1995) over a collection of customer objects, a name such as *CustomerIterator* would be appropriate.

Table 2. Example names for operations.

Initial Name	Good Analysis Name	Good Design Name	Issue
Open Acc	Open Account	openAccount()	An abbreviation was replaced with the full word to make it clear what is meant.
Mailing Label Print	Print Mailing Label	printMailingLabel()	The verb was moved to the beginning of the name to make it active.
purchaseparkingpass()	Purchase Parking Pass	purchaseParkingPass()	Mixed case was applied to increase the readability of the design-level name.
Save the Object	Save	save()	The name was shortened because the term "TheObject" did not add any value.

66. *Name Operations with a Strong Verb*

Operations implement the functionality of an object; therefore, they should be named in a manner that effectively communicates that functionality. Table 2 lists operation names for analysis class diagrams as well as for design class diagrams—the assumption being that your implementation language follows Java naming conventions (Vermeulen et al. 2000)—indicating how the operation name has been improved in each case.

67. *Name Attributes with a Domain-Based Noun*

As with classes and operations, you should use full descriptions to name your attribute so that it is obvious what the attribute represents. Table 3 suggests a Java-based naming convention for analysis names that are in the *Attribute Name* format, although *attribute name* and *Attribute name* formats are also fine if applied consistently. Table 3 also suggests design names that take an *attributeName* format, although the *attribute_name* format is just as popular depending on your implementation language.

68. *Do Not Model Scaffolding Code*

Scaffolding code includes the attributes and operations required to implement basic functionality within your classes, such as the code required to implement relationships with other classes. Scaffolding code also includes getters and setters, also known as accessors and mutators, such as *getItem()* and *setItem()* in Figure 11, that get and set the value of attributes. You can simplify your class diagrams by assuming that scaffolding code will be created (many CASE tools can generate it for you automatically) and not model it. Figure 11 depicts the difference between the *OrderItem* class without scaffolding code and with it—including the constructor, the common static operation *findAllInstances()* that all business classes implement (in this system), and the attributes *item* and *order*

Table 3. Example names for attributes.

Initial Name	Good Analysis Name	Good Design Name	Issue
fName	First Name	firstName	Do not use abbreviations in attribute names.
firstname	First Name	firstName	Capitalizing the second word of the design name makes the attribute name easier to read.
personFirstName	First Name	firstName	This depends on the context of the attribute, but if this is an attribute of the "Person" class, then including "person" merely lengthens the name without providing any value.
nameLast	Last Name	lastName	The name "nameLast" was not consistent with "firstName" (and it sounded strange anyway).
hTTPConnection	HTTP Connection	httpConnection	The abbreviation for the design name should be in all lowercase.
firstNameString	First Name	firstName	Indicating the type of the attribute, in this case "string," couples the attribute name to its type. If the type changes, perhaps because you decide to reimplement this attribute as an instance of the class "NameString," then you would need to rename the attribute.
OrderItemCollection	Order Items	orderItems	The second version of the design name is shorter and easier to understand.

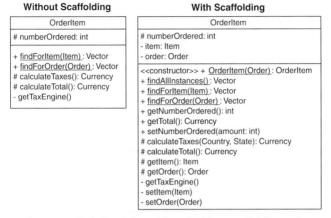

Figure 11. OrderItem class with and without scaffolding code.

and their corresponding getters and setters to maintain its relationships with the *Order* class and *Item* class, respectively.

69. Do Not Model Keys

A key is a unique identifier of a data entity or table. Unless you are using a UML class diagram to model the logical or physical schema of a database (Ambler 2001) you should not model keys in your class. Keys are a data concept, not an object-oriented concept. A particularly common mistake by novice developers is to model foreign keys in classes, the data attributes needed to identify other rows of data within the database.

70. Never Show Classes with Just Two Compartments

It is allowable within the UML to have a class with one or more compartments. Although compartments may appear in any order, traditionally the top-most compartment indicates the name of the class and any information pertinent to the class as a whole (such as a stereotype); the second optional compartment typically lists the attributes; and the third optional compartment typically lists the operations. Other "nonstandard" compartments may be added to the class to provide information such as lists of exceptions thrown or notes pertaining to the class. Because naming conventions for attributes and operations are similar, and because people new to object development may confuse the two concepts, it isn't advisable to have classes with just two compartments (one for the class name and one listing either attributes or operations). If necessary, include a blank compartment as a placeholder, as you can see with the *Student* class in Figure 10.

71. Label Uncommon Class Compartments

If you do intend to include a class compartment that isn't one of the standard three—class name, attribute list, operations list—then include a descriptive label such as "Exceptions" or "Constraints" centered at the top of the compartment as you can see with the *Student* class in Figure 10.

72. Include an Ellipsis (...) at the End of Incomplete Lists

You know that the list of attributes of the *Student* class of Figure 10 is incomplete because of the ellipsis at the end of the list. Without the ellipsis, there would be no indication that there is more to the class than what is currently shown (Evitts 2000).

73. List Static Operations/Attributes Before Instance Operations/Attributes

Static operations and attributes typically deal with early aspects of a class's life cycle, such as the creation of objects or finding existing instances of the classes. In other words, when you are working with a class you often start with statics. Therefore it makes sense to list them first in their appropriate compartments as you can see in Figure 11 (statics are underlined).

74. List Operations/Attributes in Decreasing Visibility

The greater the visibility of an operation or attribute, the greater the chance that someone else will be interested in it. For example, because public operations are accessible to a greater audience than protected operations, there is a greater likelihood that greater interest exists in public operations. Therefore, list your attributes and operations in order of decreasing visibility so that they appear in order of importance. As you can see in Figure 11, the operations and attributes of the *OrderItem* class are then listed alphabetically for each level of visibility.

75. For Parameters That Are Objects, List Only Their Type

As you can see in Figure 11, operation signatures can become quite long, extending the size of the class symbol. To save space, you can forgo listing the types of objects that are passed as parameters to operations. For example, Figure 11 lists *calculateTaxes(Country, State)* instead of *calculateTaxes(country: Country, state: State)*, thus saving space.

76. Develop Consistent Operation and Attribute Signatures

Operation names should be consistent with one another. For example, in Figure 11, all finder operations start with the text *find*. Parameter names should also be consistent with one another. For example, parameter names such as *theFirstName*, *firstName*, and *firstNm* are not consistent with one another, nor are *firstName*, *aPhoneNumber*, and *theStudentNumber*. Pick one naming style for your parameters and stick to it. Similarly, be consistent also in the order of parameters. For example, the methods *doSomething(securityToken, startDate)* and *doSomethingElse(studentNumber, securityToken)* could be made more consistent by always passing *securityToken* as either the first or the last parameter.

+ findAllInstances(): Vector
{exceptions=NetworkFailure, DatabaseError}

Figure 12. Indicating the exceptions thrown by an operation.

77. *Avoid Stereotypes Implied by Language Naming Conventions*

The UML allows for stereotypes to be applied to operations. In Figure 11. I, applied the stereotype <<constructor>> to the operation *OrderItem(Order),* but that information is redundant because the name of the operation implies that it's a constructor, at least if the implementation language is Java or C++. Furthermore, you should avoid stereotypes such as <<getter>> and <<setter>> for similar reasons—the names *getAttributeName()* and *setAttributeName()* indicate the type of operations you're dealing with.

78. *Indicate Exceptions in an Operation's Property String*

Some languages, such as Java, allow operations to throw exceptions to indicate that an error condition has occurred. Exceptions can be indicated with a UML property string, an example of which is shown in Figure 12.

4.3 Interface Guidelines

An interface is a collection of operation signatures and/or attribute definitions that ideally defines a cohesive set of behaviors. Interfaces are implemented, "realized" in UML parlance, by classes and components—to realize an interface, a class or component must implement the operations and attributes defined by the interface. Any given class or component may implement zero or more interfaces, and one or more classes or components can implement the same interface.

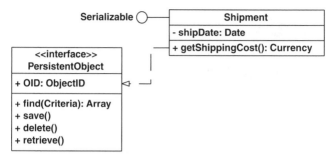

Figure 13. Interfaces on UML class diagrams.

79. *Reflect Implementation Language Constraints in Interface Definitions*

In Figure 13, you can see that a standard class box has been used to define the interface *PersistentObject* (note the use of the <<interface>> stereotype). This interface includes a public attribute named OID and several public operations. Unfortunately, it could not be implemented in Java because this language does not (yet) support instance attributes in the definition of interfaces. Therefore, you need to rework this interface definition if you wish to implement my model in Java.

80. *Name Interfaces According to Language Naming Conventions*

Interfaces are named in the same manner as classes: they have fully described names in the format *InterfaceName*. In Java it is common to have interface names such as *Serializable* that end in *able* or *ible* or just descriptive nouns such as *EJBObject*. In Microsoft environments, it is common practice to prefix interface names with a capital *I*, resulting in names such as *IComponent*.

81. Prefer "Lollipop" Notation to Indicate Realization of an Interface

As you can see in Figure 13, there are two ways to indicate that a class or component implements an interface: the lollipop notation used with the *Serializable* interface and the realization line (the dashed line with a closed arrowhead) used with the *PersistentObject* interface. The lollipop notation is preferred because it is visually compact; the class box and realization line approach tend to clutter your diagrams.

82. Define Interfaces Separately from Your Classes

To reduce clutter, you can define interfaces separately from classes, either in another diagram specifically for interface definitions or simply on one edge of your class diagram.

83. Do Not Model the Operations and Attributes of Interfaces in Your Classes

In Figure 13, you'll notice that the *Shipment* class does not include the attributes or operations defined by the two interfaces that it realizes. That information would be redundant because it is already contained within the interface definitions.

4.4 Relationship Guidelines

For ease of discussion the term relationships shall include all UML concepts such as associations, aggregation, composition, dependencies, inheritance, and realizations. In other words, if it's a line on a UML class diagram, we'll consider it a relationship.

84. Model Relationships Horizontally

With the exception of inheritance, the common convention is to depict relationships horizontally; the more consistent you are in the manner in which you render your diagrams,

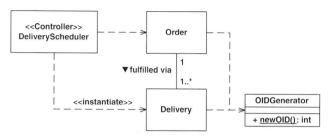

Figure 14. Shipping an order.

the easier it will be to read them. In Figure 14, you can see that the dependencies are modeled horizontally, although the fulfilled via association is not. This sometimes happens.

85. Model Collaboration Between Two Elements Only When They Have a Relationship

You need to have some sort of relationship between two model elements to enable them to collaborate. Furthermore, if two model elements do not collaborate with one another, then there is no need for a relationship between them.

86. Model a Dependency When the Relationship Is Transitory

Transitory relationships—relationships that are not persistent—occur when one or more of the items involved in a relationship is either itself transitory or a class. In Figure 14, you can see that there is a dependency between *DeliveryScheduler* and *Order*. *DeliveryScheduler* is a transitory class, one that does not need to persist in your database, and therefore, there is no need for any relationship between the scheduler and the order objects with which it interacts to persist. For the same reason, the relationship between *DeliveryScheduler* and *Delivery* is also a dependency, even though *DeliveryScheduler* creates *Delivery* objects.

In Figure 14, instances of *Delivery* interact with *OIDGenerator* to obtain a new integer value that acts as an object identifier (OID) to be used as a primary key value in a relational database (Ambler 2001). You know that *Delivery* objects are interacting with *OIDGenerator* and are not an instance of it because the operation is static. Therefore, there is no permanent relationship to be recorded, and so, a dependency is sufficient.

87. Tree-Route Similar Relationships to a Common Class

In Figure 14, you can see that both *Delivery* and *Order* have a dependency on *OIDGenerator*. Note how the two dependencies are drawn in combination in "tree configuration," instead of as two separate lines, to reduce clutter in the diagram (Evitts 2000). You can take this approach with any type of relationship. It is quite common with inheritance hierarchies (as you can see in Figure 17), as long as the relationship ends that you are combining are identical. For example, in Figure 15, you can see that *OrderItem* is involved in two separate relationships. Unfortunately, the multiplicities are different for each: one is 1..* and the other 0..*, and so, you can't combine the two into a tree structure. Had they been the same, you could have combined them, even though one relationship is aggregation and the other is association.

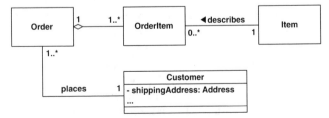

Figure 15. Modeling an order.

Table 4. UML multiplicity indicators.

Indicator	Meaning
0..1	Zero or one
1	One only
0..*	Zero or more
1..*	One or more
n	Only n (where $n > 1$)
*	Many
0..n	Zero to n (where $n > 1$)
1..n	One to n (where $n > 1$)
n..m	Where n & m both > 1
n..*	n or more, where $n > 1$

Note that there is a danger that you may be motivated to retain a relationship in order to preserve the tree arrangement when you really should change it.

88. *Always Indicate the Multiplicity*

For each class involved in a relationship, there will always be a multiplicity for it. When the multiplicity is one and one only—for example, with aggregation and composition, it is often common for the part to be involved only with one whole—many modelers will not model the "1" beside the diamond. I believe that this is a mistake, and as you can see in Figure 15, I indicate the multiplicity in this case. If the multiplicity is "1," then indicate it as such so that your readers know that you've considered the multiplicity. Table 4 summarizes the multiplicity indicators that you will see on UML class diagrams.

89. *Avoid a Multiplicity of "*"*

You should avoid the use of "*" to indicate multiplicity on a UML class diagram because your reader can never be sure if you really mean "0..*" or "1..*".

90. *Replace Relationship Lines with Attribute Types*

In Figure 15, you can see that Customer has a *shippingAddress* attribute of type *Address*—part of the scaffolding code to maintain the association between customer objects and address objects. This simplifies the diagram because it visually replaces a class box and association, although it contradicts the *Do Not Model Scaffolding Code* guideline. You will need to judge which guideline to follow, the critical issue being which one will best improve your diagram given your situation.

A good rule of thumb is that if your audience is familiar with the class, then show it as a type. For example, if *Address* is a new concept within your domain then show it as a class; if it's been around for awhile then showing it as a type should work well.

91. *Do Not Model Implied Relationships*

In Figure 15 there is an implied association between *Item* and *Order*; items appear on orders, but it was not modeled. A mistake? No, the association is implied through *OrderItem*. Orders are made up of order items, which in turn are described by items. If you model this implied association, not only do you clutter your diagram, you also run the risk that somebody will develop the additional code to maintain it. If you don't intend to maintain the actual relationship—for example, you aren't going to write the scaffolding code—then don't model it.

92. *Do Not Model Every Dependency*

Model a dependency between classes only if doing so adds to the communication value of your diagram. As always, you should strive to follow AM's (Chapter 12) practice, *Depict Models Simply*.

4.5 Association Guidelines

93. Center Names on Associations

It is common convention to center the name of an association above an association path, as you can see in Figure 15 with the *describes* association between *Order* and *Item*, or beside the path as with the *fulfilled via* association between *Order* and *Delivery* in Figure 14.

94. Write Concise Association Names in Active Voice

The name of an association, which is optional although highly recommended, is typically one or two descriptive words. If you find that an association name is wordy, think about it from the other direction; for example, the *places* name of Figure 15 is concise when read from right to left but would be wordy if written from the left-to-right perspective (e.g., "is placed by"). Furthermore, *places* is written in active voice instead of passive voice, making it clearer to the reader.

95. Indicate Directionality to Clarify an Association Name

When it isn't clear in which direction the name of an association should be read, you can indicate the direction with a filled triangle as you can see in Figure 15 between *OrderItem* and *Item*. This marker indicates that the association should be read as "an item describes an order item" instead of "an order item describes an item." It is also quite common to indicate the directionality on recursive associations, where the association starts and ends on the same class, such as *mentors* in Figure 16.

Better yet, when an association name isn't clear, you should consider rewording it or maybe even renaming the classes.

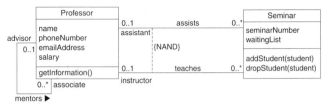

Figure 16. Professors and seminars.

96. Name Unidirectional Associations in the Same Direction

The reading direction of an association name should be the same as that of the unidirectional association. This is basically a consistency issue.

97. Word Association Names Left to Right

Because people in Western societies read from left to right, it is common practice to word association names so that they make sense when read from left to right. Had I followed this guideline with the *describes* association of Figure 15, I likely would not have needed to include the direction marker.

98. Indicate Role Names When Multiple Associations Between Two Classes Exist

Role names are optionally indicated on association ends to indicate how a class is involved in the association. Although the name of an association should make the roles of the two classes clear, it isn't always obvious when several associations exist between two classes. For example, in Figure 16, there are two associations between *Professor* and *Seminar*: *assists* and *teaches*. These two association names reflect common terminology at the university and cannot be changed. Therefore we opt to indicate the roles that professors play in each association to clarify them.

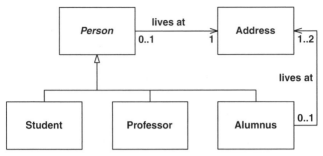

Figure 17. Modeling people in a university.

99. Indicate Role Names on Recursive Associations

Role names can be used to clarify recursive associations, ones that involve the same class on both ends, as you can see with the *mentors* association in Figure 16. The diagram clearly depicts the concept that an advisor mentors zero or more associate professors.

100. Make Associations Bi-Directional Only When Collaboration Occurs in Both Directions

The *lives at* association between *Person* and *Address* in Figure 17 is unidirectional. A person object knows its address, but an address object does not know who lives at it. Within this domain, there is no requirement to traverse the association from *Address* to *Person*; therefore, the association does not need to be bi-directional (two-way). This reduces the code that needs to be written and tested within the address class because the scaffolding to maintain the association to *Person* isn't required.

101. Redraw Inherited Associations Only When Something Changes

An interesting aspect of Figure 17 is the association between *Person* and *Address*. First, this association was pushed up to

Person because *Professor, Student,* and *Alumnus* all had a *lives at* association with *Address.* Because associations are implemented by the combination of attributes and operations, both of which are inherited, the implication is that associations are inherited. If the nature of the association doesn't change—for example, both students and professors live at only one address—then we don't have any reason to redraw the association. However, because the association between *Alumnus* and *Address* is different, we have a requirement to track one or two addresses, and so, we needed to redraw the association to reflect this.

102. Question Multiplicities Involving Minimums and Maximums

The problem with minimums and maximums is that they change over time. For example, today you may have a business rule that states an alumnus has either one or two addresses that the university tracks, motivating you to model the multiplicity as 1..2, as depicted in Figure 17. However, if you build your system to reflect this rule, then when the rule changes you may find that you have significant rework to perform. In most object languages, it is easier to implement a 1..* multiplicity or, better yet, a 0..* multiplicity, because you don't have to check the size of the collection maintaining the association. Providing greater flexibility with less code seems good to me.

4.6 Inheritance Guidelines

Inheritance models "is a" and "is like" relationships, enabling you to easily reuse existing data and code. When *A* inherits from *B,* we say that *A* is the subclass of *B* and that *B* is the superclass of *A.* Furthermore, we say that we have "pure inheritance" when *A* inherits all of the attributes and methods of *B.* The UML modeling notation for inheritance is a line with a closed arrowhead pointing from the subclass to the superclass.

103. Apply the Sentence Rule for Inheritance

One of the following sentences should make sense: "A subclass IS A superclass" or "A subclass IS KIND OF A superclass." For example, it makes sense to say that a student is a person, but it does not make sense to say that a student is an address or is like an address, and so, the class *Student* likely should not inherit from *Address*—association is likely a better option, as you can see in Figure 17. If it does not make sense to say that "the subclass is a superclass" or at least "the subclass is kind of a superclass," then you are likely misapplying inheritance.

104. Place Subclasses Below Superclasses

It is common convention to place a subclass, such as *Student* in Figure 17, below its superclass—*Person* in this case. Evitts (2000) says it well: Inheritance goes up.

105. Beware of Data-Based Inheritance

If the only reason why two classes inherit from each other is because they share common data attributes, then this indicates one of two things: you have either missed some common behavior (this is likely if the sentence rule applies) or you should have applied association instead.

106. A Subclass Should Inherit Everything

A subclass should inherit all of the attributes and operations of its superclass, and therefore all of its relationships as well—a concept called pure inheritance. The advantage of pure inheritance is that you only have to understand what a subclass inherits, and not what it does not inherit. Although this sounds trivial, in a deep class hierarchy it makes it a lot easier if you only need to understand what each class adds, and not what it takes away. Larman (2002) calls this the "100% rule." Note that this contradicts the *Redraw Inherited Associations Only When Something Changes* guideline, and so, you'll need to decide accordingly.

4.7 Aggregation and Composition Guidelines

Sometimes an object is made up of other objects. For example, an airplane is made up of a fuselage, wings, engines, landing gear, flaps, and so on. A delivery shipment contains one or more packages. A team consists of two or more employees. These are all examples of the concept of aggregation, which represents "is part of" relationships. An engine is part of a plane, a package is part of a shipment, and an employee is part of a team. Aggregation is a specialization of association, specifying a whole–part relationship between two objects. Composition is a stronger form of aggregation, where the whole and the parts have coincident lifetimes, and it is very common for the whole to manage the life cycle of its parts. From a stylistic point of view, because aggregation and composition are both specializations of association, the guidelines for associations apply.

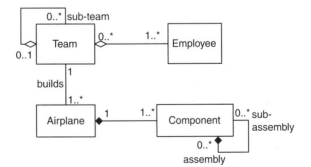

Figure 18. Examples of aggregation and composition.

107. Apply the Sentence Rule for Aggregation

It should make sense to say "the part IS PART OF the whole." For example, in Figure 18, it makes sense to say that an employee is part of a team or that a component is part of an airplane. However, it does not make sense to say that a team is part of an airplane or an airplane is part of a team—but it does make sense to say that a team builds airplanes, an indication that association is applicable.

108. Be Interested in Both the Whole and the Part

For aggregation and composition, you should be interested in both the whole and the part separately—both the whole and the part should exhibit behavior that is of value to your system. For example, you could model the fact that my watch has hands on it, but if this fact isn't pertinent to your system (perhaps you sell watches but not watch parts), then there is no value in modeling watch hands.

109. Place the Whole to the Left of the Part

It is common convention to draw the whole, such as *Team* and *Airplane*, to the left of the part, *Employee* and *Component,* respectively.

110. Apply Composition to Aggregates of Physical Items

Composition is usually applicable whenever aggregation is AND when both classes represent physical items. For example, in Figure 18 you can see that composition is used between *Airplane* and *Component,* whereas aggregation is used between *Team* and *Employee*—airplanes and components are both physical items, whereas teams are not.

111. Apply Composition When the Parts Share Their Persistence Life Cycle with the Whole

If the persistence life cycle of the parts is the same as the whole, if they're read at the same time, if they're saved at the same time, if they're deleted at the same time, then composition is likely applicable.

112. Don't Worry About the Diamonds

When deciding whether to use aggregation or composition over association, Craig Larman (2002) says it best: "If in doubt, leave it out." The reality is that many modelers will agonize over when to use aggregation when the reality is that there is very little difference between association, aggregation, and composition at the coding level.

5.

Package Diagrams

A "package diagram" is any UML diagram, commonly a UML use case diagram or UML class diagram, composed only of packages. A package is a UML construct that enables you to organize model elements, such as use cases or classes, into groups. Packages are depicted as file folders and can be applied on any UML diagram. Although package diagrams are not official UML diagrams, their creation is common enough in practice to warrant discussion. Create a package diagram to

- depict a high-level overview of your requirements,
- depict a high-level overview of your design,
- logically modularize a complex diagram,
- organize source code, or
- model a framework (Evitts 2000).

5.1 Class Package Diagram Guidelines

113. Create Class Package Diagrams to Logically Organize Your Design

Figure 19 depicts a UML class diagram organized into packages. In addition to the package guidelines presented later in this chapter, apply the following heuristics to organize UML class diagrams into package diagrams:

- Classes of a framework belong in the same package.
- Classes in the same inheritance hierarchy typically belong in the same package.

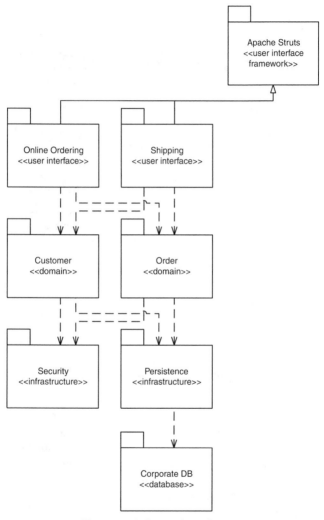

Figure 19. A class package diagram.

- Classes related to one another via aggregation or composition often belong in the same package.
- Classes that collaborate with each other a lot often belong in the same package.

114. Create UML Component Diagrams to Physically Organize Your Design

If you have decided on a component-based approach to design, such as that promoted by Enterprise Java Beans (EJB) (Roman et al. 2002) or Visual Basic, you should prefer a UML component diagram over a package diagram to depict your physical design. A version of Figure 19 as a UML component diagram is presented in Chapter 10 and, as you can see, that diagram is better suited for a physical design. Always remember to follow Agile Modeling's (Chapter 12) *Apply the Right Artifact(s)* practice.

115. Place Inheriting Packages Below Base Packages

Inheritance between packages is depicted in Figure 19 and, as you can see, the inheriting package is shown below the base package. This approach is consistent with other inheritance guidelines.

116. Vertically Layer Class Package Diagrams

Dependencies between packages indicate that the contents of the dependent package depend on, or have structural knowledge of, the contents of the other package. In Figure 19, the packages are placed on the diagram to reflect the logical layering of your architecture. The user interface interacts with domain classes, which in turn use infrastructure classes, some of which access the database—which is traditionally depicted in a top-down manner.

5.2 Use Case Package Diagram Guidelines

Use cases are a primary requirement artifact in many object-oriented development methodologies. This is particularly true of instantiations of the Unified Process (Rational Corporation 2002; Ambler 2000). For larger projects, package diagrams are often created to organize these usage requirements.

117. Create Use Case Package Diagrams to Organize Your Requirements

In addition to the package guidelines presented below, apply the following heuristics to organize UML use case diagrams into package diagrams:

- Keep associated use cases together: included, extending, and inheriting use cases belong in the same package as the base/parent use case.
- Group use cases on the basis of needs of the main actors. For example, in Figure 20, the *Enrollment* package contains use cases pertinent to enrolling students in seminars, a vital collection of services provided by the university.

118. Include Actors on Use Case Package Diagrams

Including actors on package diagrams helps to put the packages in context, making diagrams easier to understand.

119. Horizontally Arrange Use Case Package Diagrams

The primary audience of Use Case package diagrams is project stakeholders; therefore, the organization of these diagrams should reflect their needs. The packages in Figure 20 are arranged horizontally, with dependencies drawn from left to right to reflect the direction that people in Western cultures read.

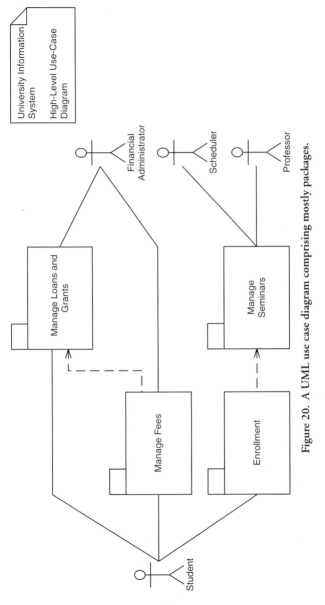

University Information System

High-Level Use-Case Diagram

Figure 20. A UML use case diagram comprising mostly packages.

57

5.3 Package Guildelines

The advice presented in this section is applicable to packages on any UML diagram, not just package diagrams.

120. Give Packages Simple, Descriptive Names

In both Figure 19 and Figure 20, the packages have simple, descriptive names, such as *Shipping, Customer, Enrollment,* and *Manage Loans, and Grants,* which make it very clear what the package encapsulates.

121. Make Packages Cohesive

Anything that you put into a package should make sense when considered with the rest of the package contents. A good test to determine whether a package is cohesive is whether you can give your package a short, descriptive name. If you can't, then you likely have put several unrelated things into the package.

122. Indicate Architectural Layers with Stereotypes on Packages

It is very common to organize your design into architectural layers such as user interface, business/domain, persistence/data, and infrastructure/system. In Figure 19 you see that stereotypes such as <<user interface>>, <<domain>>, <<infrastructure>>, and <<database>> have been applied to packages.

123. Avoid Cyclic Dependencies Between Packages

Knoernschild (2002) advises that you avoid the situation in which package A is dependent on package B which is dependent on package C which in turn is dependent on package A—in this case, $A \rightarrow B \rightarrow C \rightarrow A$ forms a cycle. Because these packages are coupled to one another, they will be harder to test, maintain, and enhance over time. Cyclic dependencies are a good indicator that you need to refactor one or more packages, removing the elements from them that are causing the cyclic dependency.

124. *Reflect Internal Relationships in Package Dependencies*

When one package depends on another, it implies that there are one or more relationships between the contents of the two packages. For example, if it's a use case package diagram, then there is likely an include, extend, or inheritance relationship between a use case in one package and one in the other package.

6.

UML Sequence

Diagrams

UML sequence diagrams are a dynamic modeling technique, as are UML collaboration diagrams. UML sequence diagrams are typically used to

- validate and flesh out the logic and completeness of a usage scenario. A usage scenario is exactly what its name indicates—the description of a way that your system could be used. The logic of a usage scenario may be part of a use case, perhaps an alternate course; one entire pass through a use case, such as the logic described by the basic course of action or a portion of the basic course of action plus one or more alternate scenarios; or a pass through the logic contained in several use cases, for example, when a student enrolls in the university and then immediately enrolls in three seminars.
- explore your design because they provide a way for you to visually step through invocation of the operations defined by your classes.
- give you a feel for which classes in your application are going to be complex, which in turn is an indication that you may need to draw state chart diagrams for those classes.
- detect bottlenecks within an object-oriented design. By looking at what messages are being sent to an object, and by looking at roughly how long it takes to run the invoked

method, you quickly get an understanding of where you need to change your design to distribute the load within your system. Naturally, you will still want to gather telemetry data from a profiling tool to detect the exact location of your bottlenecks.

6.1 General Guidelines

125. *Strive for Left-to-Right Ordering of Messages*

You start the message flow of a sequence diagram in the top-left corner; a message that appears lower in the diagram is sent after one that appears above it. Because people in Western cultures read from left to right, you should strive to arrange the classifiers (actors, classes, objects, and use cases) across the top of your diagram in such a way as to depict message flow from left to right. In Figure 21, you can see that the classifiers have been arranged exactly this way; had the *Seminar* object been to the left of the controller, this would not have been the case. Sometimes it isn't possible for all messages to flow from left to right; for example, it is common for pairs of objects to invoke operations on each other.

126. *Layer Classifiers*

Layering is a common approach to object-oriented design. It is quite common for systems to be organized into user interface, process/controller, business, persistence, and system layers (Ambler 2001). When systems are designed in this fashion, classifiers within each layer usually collaborate closely with one another and are relatively decoupled from the other layers. It makes sense to layer your sequence diagrams in a similar manner. One such layering approach is to start with the upper layers, such as your user interface, on the left-hand side and work through to the lower layers as you move to the right. Layering your sequence diagrams in this manner will often

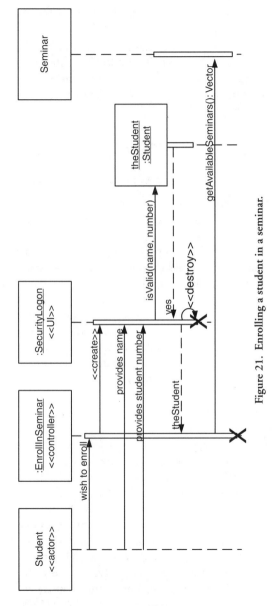

Figure 21. Enrolling a student in a seminar.

make them easier to read and will also make it easier to find layering logic problems. Figure 21 takes such an approach.

127. Give an Actor the Same Name as a Class, if Necessary

In Figure 21 you can see that there is an actor named *Student* and a class named *Student*. This is perfectly fine because the two classifiers represent two different concepts: the actor represents the student in the real world whereas the class represents the student within the business application that you are building.

128. Include a Prose Description of the Logic

Figure 21 can be hard to follow, particularly for people not familiar with reading sequence diagrams, because it is very close to actual source code. It is quite common to include a business description of the logic you are modeling, particularly when the sequence diagram depicts a usage scenario, in the left-hand margin, as you can see in Figure 22. This increases the understandability of your diagram, and as Rosenberg and Scott (1999) point out this also provides valuable traceability information between your use cases and sequence diagrams.

129. Place Proactive System Actors on the Left-Most Side of Your Diagram

Proactive system actors—actors that initiate interaction with yours—are often the focus of what you are modeling. For business applications the primary actor for most usage scenarios is a person or organization who initiates the scenario being modeled.

130. Place Reactive System Actors on the Right-Most Side of Your Diagram

Reactive system actors—systems that initiate interaction with yours—should be placed on the right-most side of

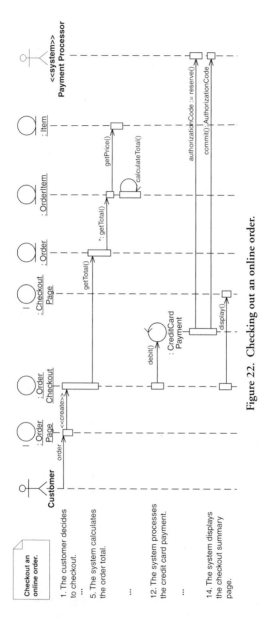

Figure 22. Checking out an online order.

your diagram because, for many business applications, these actors are treated as "back-end entities," that is, things that your system interacts with through access techniques such as C APIs, CORBA IDL, message queues, or Web services. In other words, put back-end systems at the back end of your diagrams.

131. *Avoid Modeling Object Destruction*

Although memory management issues are important and, in particular, the removal of an object from memory at the right time, many modelers choose not to bother modeling object destruction on sequence diagrams (via an X at the bottom of an activation box or via a message with the <<destroy>> stereotype). Compare Figure 21 with Figure 22. Notice how object destruction introduces clutter into Figure 21 without any apparent benefit, yet Figure 22 gets along without indicating object destruction. Remember to follow Agile Modeling's (AM) (Chapter 12) practice *Depict Models Simply.*

Note that, in real-time systems, memory management is often such a critical issue that you may in fact decide to model object destruction.

132. *Don't Sweat Activation Boxes*

Activation boxes are the little rectangles on the dashed lines hanging down from classifiers on UML sequence diagrams. Activation boxes are optional and are used to indicate focus of control, implying where and how much processing occurs. However, activation boxes are little better than visual noise because memory management issues are better left in the hands of programmers. Some modelers prefer the "continuous style" used in Figure 21, where the activation boxes remain until processing ends. Others prefer the "broken style" used in Figure 22. Both styles are fine. Choose one and move forward.

6.2 Classifier Guidelines

Note that naming conventions for classifiers are described elsewhere: in Chapter 3 for use cases, in Chapter 4 for classes and interfaces, and in Chapter 10 for components.

133. Name Objects When You Reference Them in Messages

Objects on sequence diagrams have labels in the standard UML format "*name: ClassName*" where "name" is optional (objects that have a name are called named objects, whereas those without names are called anonymous objects). In Figure 21 the instance of *Student* was given the name *theStudent* because it is referred to as a return value to a message, whereas the instance of the *SecurityLogon* class did not need to be referenced anywhere else in the diagram and thus could be anonymous.

134. Name Objects When Several of the Same Type Exist

Whenever a sequence diagram includes several objects of the same type—for example, in Figure 23, you can see that there are two instances of the class *Account*—you should give all objects of that type a name to make your diagram unambiguous.

135. Apply Textual Stereotypes to Classifiers Consistently

Table 5 summarizes common stereotypes that you may want to consider applying to classifiers on sequence diagrams. Don't invest a lot of time agonizing over which stereotypes you should use—for example, <<JSP>> and <<java server page>> are both fine—just choose one and apply it consistently.

136. Apply Visual Stereotypes Sparingly

You can apply visual stereotypes on your sequence diagrams, as in Figure 22 and Figure 23, but it is not a common practice and therefore may reduce the understandability of your

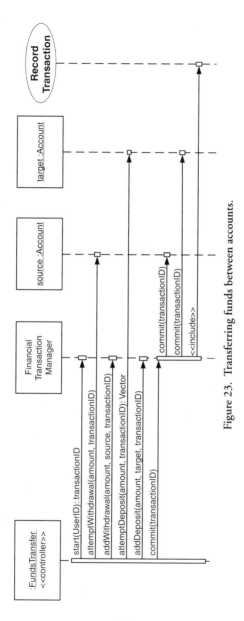

Figure 23. Transferring funds between accounts.

67

Table 5. Common Stereotypes.

Stereotype	Usage
<<ASP>>	During design to represent a Microsoft Active Server Page.
<<component>>	During design to indicate a component.
<<controller>>	To indicate a controller class that implements business logic pertaining to a usage scenario and/or logic that involves several business classes.
<<GUI>>	During design to represent a graphical user interface screen.
<<HTML>>	During design to represent an HTML page.
<<interface>>	During design to represent a Java interface.
<<JSP>>	During design to represent a Java Server Page.
<<report>>	During design to represent a printed or electronic report.
<<system>>	To indicate system actors.
<<user interface>>	For a generic user interface class, typically used on an analysis-level diagram where you haven't yet decided on an implementation platform.

diagrams. In Figure 22, *Customer* is an actor (using the same notation as use case diagrams), *OrderCheckout* is a controller class, *CheckoutPage* is a user interface class, and *Order* is a business entity class.

Note that visual stereotypes are commonly used by teams that develop robustness diagrams (Rosenberg and Scott 1999; Ambler 2002) because these diagrams use the visual stereotypes depicted in Figure 22 and therefore everyone involved with your project is accustomed to this notation.

137. Focus on Critical Interactions
The AM practice *Create Simple Content* advises you to focus on the critical aspects of your system when you are creating

a model and not to include extraneous details. Therefore, if your sequence diagram is exploring business logic, then you don't need to include the detailed interactions that your objects have with your database. Messages such as *save()* and *delete()* may be sufficient or, better yet, you could simply assume that persistence will happen appropriately and not even go to that level of detail. In Figure 22 there isn't any logic for reading orders and order items from the database or object cache. Nor do you see logic for the *CreditCardPayment* class to connect to the payment processor, but that surely must be happening in the background. By focusing only on the critical interactions—those that are pertinent to what you are modeling—you keep your diagrams as simple as possible but still get the job done, thus increasing your productivity as a modeler and very likely increasing the readability of your diagrams.

6.3 Message Guidelines

Note that naming conventions for operation signatures—guidelines that are pertinent to naming messages, parameters, and return values—are described in detail in Chapter 4.

138. *Justify Message Names Beside the Arrowhead*

Most modelers will justify message names, such as *calculate Total()* in Figure 22, so that they are aligned with the arrowhead. The general idea is that the receiver of the message will implement the corresponding operation, and so, it makes sense that the message name be close to that classifier.

Notice that in Figure 23 this guideline was not followed. All of the message names are aligned so that they are beside the end of the arrow, putting them close to the sender. The advantage of this approach is that it is very easy to see the logic of the scenario being modeled. The disadvantage is that it can be difficult to determine which operation is being invoked on the classifiers on the right-hand side of the diagram because you need to follow the lines across to the invocation box. As usual, pick one approach and apply it consistently.

139. Create Objects Directly

There are two common ways to indicate object creation on a sequence diagram: send a message with the <<create>> stereotype as shown in Figure 22 with *OrderCheckout*, or directly show creation by dropping the classifier down in your diagram and invoking a message into its side, as you can see with *theStudent* in Figure 21 and *CreditCardPayment* in Figure 22. The primary advantage of the direct approach is that it visually communicates that the object doesn't exist until part way through the logic being modeled.

140. Apply Operation Signatures for Software Messages

Whenever a message is sent to a software-based classifier— such as a class, an interface, or a component—it is common convention to depict the message name using the syntax of your implementation language. For example, in Figure 23 the message *commit(transactionID)* is sent to the source account object.

141. Apply Prose for Messages Involving Human and Organization Actors

Whenever the source or target of a message is an actor representing a person or organization, the message is labeled with brief prose describing the information being communicated. For example, in Figure 21 the "messages" sent by the student actor are *provides name* and *provides student number*, descriptions of what the actual person is doing.

142. Prefer Names Over Types for Parameters

Notice that, in Figure 23, for most message parameters the names of parameters and not their types[3] are shown, the only exception being the *UserID* parameter being passed in the *start()* message, which enables you to identify exactly what value is being passed in the message; sometimes type information is not enough. For example, the message *addDeposit(amount, target, transactionID)* conveys more information than *addDeposit(Currency, Account, int)*. Type information for operations are better captured in UML class diagrams.

143. Indicate Types as Parameter Placeholders

Sometimes the exact information that is being passed as a parameter isn't pertinent to what you are modeling, although the fact that something is being passed is pertinent. In this case, indicate the type of the parameter, as you can see in *start(UserID)* in Figure 23.

144. Apply the `<<include>>` Stereotype for Use Case Invocations

Figure 23 shows how a use case may be invoked in a sequence diagram, via a message with the `<<include>>` stereotype, a handy trick when you're modeling a usage scenario that includes a step in which a use case is directly invoked.

6.4 Return Value Guidelines

145. Do Not Model Obvious Return Values

Return values are optionally indicated using a dashed arrow with a label indicating the return value. For example, in

---

[3] This diagram follows Java naming conventions where the names of types (classes and interfaces) start with an upper-case letter, whereas the names of parameters start with a lower-case letter.

Figure 21 the return value *theStudent* is indicated coming back from the *SecurityLogon* class as the result of invoking a message, whereas in Figure 22 no return value is indicated as the result of sending the message *getTotal()* to the order. In the first case, it isn't obvious that the act of creating a security logon object will result in the generation of a student object, whereas the return value of asking an order for its total is obvious.

146. Model a Return Value Only When You Need to Refer to It Elsewhere on a Diagram

If you need to refer to a return value elsewhere in your sequence diagram, often as a parameter passed in another message, indicate the return value on your diagram to explicitly show where it comes from.

147. Justify Return Values Beside the Arrowhead

Most modelers will justify return values, such as *yes* and *theStudent* in Figure 21 so that they are aligned with the arrowhead. The general idea is that the receiver of the return value will use it for something, and so, it makes sense that the return value be close to the receiver.

148. Model Return Values as Part of a Method Invocation

Instead of cluttering your diagram with dashed lines, consider indicating the return value in the message name instead, using the notation *returnValue := message(parameters)* that you can see applied in Figure 22 with the *authorizationCode := reserve()* message. With this approach, you have only the single message line instead of a message line and a return-value line.

149. Indicate Types as Return-Value Placeholders

Sometimes the exact information that is being returned isn't pertinent to what you are modeling, although the fact that something is being returned is important. In this case, indicate

the type of the return value, as you can see in *commit():
AuthorizationCode* in Figure 22.

150. Indicate the Actual Value for Simple Return Values

In Figure 21 the value *yes* is returned in response to the
isValid( ) message, making it very clear that the student name
and number combination was valid. Had the return value been
named *Boolean*, thus indicating the type of answer, or *eligibil-
ityIndicator*, thus indicating the name of the return value, it
would not have been as clear.

7.

UML Collaboration

Diagrams

UML collaboration diagrams, like UML sequence diagrams, are used to explore the dynamic nature of your software. Collaboration diagrams show the message flow between objects in an object-oriented application, and also imply the basic associations (relationships) between classes. Collaboration diagrams are often used to

- provide a bird's eye view of a collection of collaborating objects, particularly within a real-time environment,
- allocate functionality to classes by exploring the behavioral aspects of a system,
- model the logic of the implementation of a complex operation, particularly one that interacts with a large number of other objects, or
- explore the roles that objects take within a system, as well as the different relationships in which they are involved when in those roles.

7.1 General Guidelines

151. Create Instance-Level Diagrams to Explore Object Design Issues

Instance-level UML collaboration diagrams, such as the one shown in Figure 24, depict interactions between objects

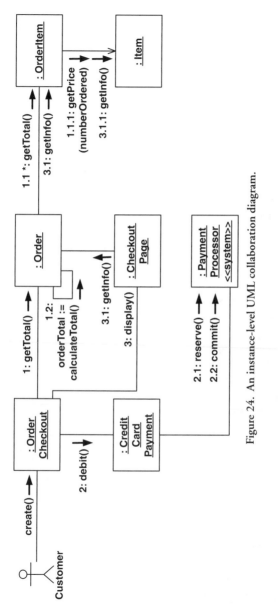

Figure 24. An instance-level UML collaboration diagram.

75

(instances). Instance-level diagrams are typically created to explore the internal design of object-oriented software. This by far is the most common style of UML collaboration diagram.

152. Create Specification-Level Diagrams to Explore Roles

Specification-level UML collaboration diagrams, such as the one shown in Figure 27 are used to analyze and explore the roles taken by domain classes within a system. This style of UML collaboration diagram is not common because most modelers identify roles via UML class diagrams.

153. Do Not Use Collaboration Diagrams to Model Process Flow

UML collaboration diagrams model interactions between objects, and objects interact by invoking messages on each other. If you want to model process or data flow, then you should consider drawing a UML activity diagram. In other words, follow the Agile Modeling (AM) (Chapter 12) practice *Apply the Right Artifact(s)*.

154. Create a Sequence Diagram When Sequence is Important

Although it is possible to indicate the sequence of message sends on a collaboration diagram, as you can see in Figure 24, the need to do this is a good indication that you should consider creating a UML sequence diagram instead. Once again, follow the AM practice *Apply the Right Artifact(s)*.

155. Apply Sequence Diagram Guidelines to Instance-Level Collaboration Diagrams

Because UML collaboration diagrams depict an alternate view of the same information as UML sequence diagrams, much of the same style advice applies. The following list of guidelines, originally presented for UML sequence diagrams, are applicable to collaboration diagrams:

- Name Objects When You Reference Them in Messages.
- Name Objects When Several of the Same Type Exist.
- Apply Textual Stereotypes to Classifiers Consistently.
- Apply Visual Stereotypes Sparingly.
- Focus on Critical Interactions.
- Prefer Names Over Types for Parameters.
- Indicate Types as Parameter Placeholders.
- Do Not Model Obvious Return Values.
- Model a Return Value Only When You Need to Refer to It Elsewhere on a Diagram.
- Model Return Values as Part of a Method Invocation.
- Indicate Types as Return-Value Placeholders.

7.2 Message Guidelines

Figure 25 presents the notation for invoking messages on UML collaboration diagrams. For example, in Figure 24 the message *1.2: orderTotal := calculateTotal()* indicates a sequence number of 1.2, there is no loop occurring, and there is a return value of *orderTotal* and an invoked method named *calculateTotal()*.

156. Indicate Parameters Only When They Aren't Clear

In Figure 24, you can see that the *1.1.1: getPrice (number Ordered)* message includes a parameter, whereas the *2: debit()* message does not, even though a *CreditCard* object is likely

sequenceNumber loopIndicator: returnValue :=
methodName(parameters)

Figure 25. Semantics for invoking a message on a collaboration diagram.

being passed as a parameter. The first message would not have been clear without the parameter, presumably because the item price changes depending on the number ordered. The second message, however, did not need the additional information for you to understand what must be happening.

157. Depict an Arrow for Each Message

In Figure 24 two messages are sent to *OrderItem* objects—*getTotal()* and *getInfo()*—and as you can see, two arrows are modeled, one for each. This makes it easy to visually determine the amount of message flow to a given object, and thus to judge the potential coupling with which it is involved, often an important consideration for refactoring (Fowler 1999) your design.

158. Consolidate Getter Invocations

It is good design practice (Ambler 2001) to make your attributes private and require other objects to obtain and modify their values by invoking getter and setter operations, respectively—for example, *getFirstName()* and *setFirstName()* on a person object. Showing these sorts of interactions on a UML collaboration diagram can be tedious, and so, you should do it only if it is absolutely necessary. When you have to invoke several getters in a row, a good shortcut is to model a single message, such as *getInfo()* in Figure 24, to act as a placeholder. Similarly, you should consider doing the same for setters with *setInfo()*. This guideline is appropriate when you are hand sketching on a whiteboard, although if you are using a CASE tool, you are likely to better model each interaction, but not show it.

If you discover that it is very common to get or set several attributes at once on an object, you may want to consider introducing a single operation to do so. These operations are called "bulk getters" and "bulk setters."

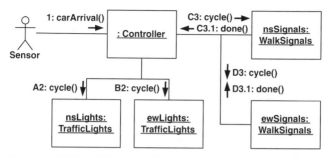

Figure 26. UML collaboration diagram depicting concurrent message invocations.

159. Indicate Concurrent Threads with Letters

Indicate concurrent threads of execution in a UML collaboration diagram by having letters precede the sequence number on messages (Douglass 1999). For example, in Figure 26 you can see that some messages are preceded by the letters *A*, *B*, *C*, and *D*, indicating that those messages are being processed concurrently. There are two concurrent threads depicted, the *AB* thread and the *CD* thread. You know this because the *A* and *B* messages share the sequence number 2 and the *C* and *D* messages share *the* sequence number 3.

7.3 Link Guidelines

The lines between the classifiers depicted on a UML collaboration diagram represent instances of the relationships—including associations, aggregations, compositions, and dependencies—between classifiers.

160. Model "Bare" Links on Instance-Level Collaboration Diagrams

As you can see in Figure 24, relationship details—such as the multiplicities, the association roles, or the name of the relationship—typically are not modeled on links within

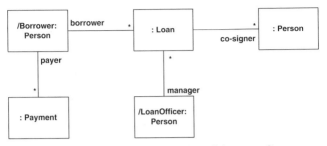

Figure 27. A Specification-Level UML collaboration diagram.

instance-level UML collaboration diagrams. Instead, this information is depicted on UML class diagrams.

161. Show Role-Pertinent Information on Specification-Level Diagrams

In Figure 27 you can see that the roles taken by classes as well as the high-level multiplicities (either blank or an asterisk to represent many) are depicted. This is the minimal information required to explore the nature of the roles taken by the domain objects; anything more, such as the exact details of the multiplicities, is better modeled on a UML class diagram. Follow the Agile Modeling practice *Depict Models Simply*.

162. Prefer Roles on Links Instead of Within Classes

In Figure 27, you can see that roles are indicated using two styles, on links and within a class. The link-based approach (e.g., *payer* on the *Person* class) is more common than the class-based role notation (e.g., */Borrower* on *Person*). Although you will need to take both approaches—for example, the use of the */LoanOfficer* role on *Person* is a great way to provide traceability to a use case diagram containing an actor of the same name—your preference should be to model roles on links because that is consistent with how roles are modeled on UML class diagrams. There is little value in modeling it in both places, as you can see with *borrower* and */Borrower* and arguably with *manager* and */LoanOfficer.*

163. Indicate Navigability Sparingly

Although it is possible to model navigation, as you can see between *OrderItem* and *Item* in Figure 24, it isn't common because it is too easily confused with message flow and it is better depicted on UML class diagrams. Indicate navigability on UML collaboration diagrams to help clarify what you are modeling.

164. Use Links to Reflect Consistent Static Relationships

The links on a UML collaboration diagram must reflect the relationships between classes within your UML class diagrams. The only way for one object to collaborate with another is for it to know about that other object. This implies that there must be an association, aggregation, or composition relationship between the two classes—a dependency relationship or an implied relationship. Sometimes it is difficult to validate the consistency between your diagrams, particularly if your UML class diagrams do not model all of the dependencies or implied relationships. For example, if an *Item* object is passed as a parameter to a *TaxCalculator* object, then there is now a dependency between these two classes, even though it might not be explicitly modeled.

8.

UML State Chart

Diagrams

UML state chart diagrams depict the dynamic behavior of an entity based on its response to events, showing how the entity reacts to various events based on its current state. Create a UML state chart diagram to

- explore the complex behavior of a class, actor, subsystem, or component, or
- model real-time systems.

8.1 General Guidelines

165. Create a State Chart When Behavior Differs Based on State

Agile Modeling's (AM) (Chapter 12) principle of *Maximize Stakeholder Investment* advises you to create a model only when it provides positive value to your efforts. If an entity, such as a class or a component, exhibits the same sort of behavior regardless of its current state, then drawing a UML state chart diagram will be of little use. For example, a *SurfaceAddress* class is fairly simple, representing data that you will display and manipulate in your system. Therefore, a UML state chart diagram would not reveal anything of interest. On the other hand, a *Seminar* object is fairly complex, reacting to events

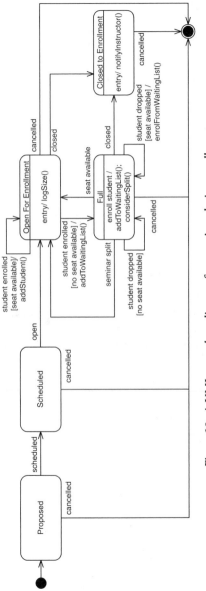

Figure 28. A UML state chart diagram for a seminar during enrollment.

83

such as enrolling a student differently depending on its current state, as you can see in Figure 28.

166. *Place the Initial State in the Top-Left Corner*

An initial state is modeled with a filled in circle, as you can see in Figure 28. Placing an initial state in the top-left corner reflects the way that people in Western cultures read.

167. *Place the Final State in the Bottom-Right Corner*

A final state is modeled with a filled in circle with a border around it, as you can see in Figure 28. Placing the final state in the bottom-right corner reflects the left-to-right, top-to-bottom approach to reading within Western cultures.

8.2 State Guidelines

A state is a stage in the behavior pattern of an entity. States are represented by the values of the attributes of an entity. For example, in Figure 28 a seminar is in the *Open For Enrollment* state when it has been flagged as open and there are seats available to be filled.

168. *State Names Should Be Simple but Descriptive*

State names such as *Open For Enrollment* and *Proposed* are easy to understand, thus increasing the communication value of Figure 28. Ideally, state names should also be written in present tense, although names such as *Proposed* (past tense) are better than *Is Proposed* (present tense).

169. *Question "Black-Hole" States*

A black-hole state is one that has transitions into it but none out of it, something that should be true only of final states. This is an indication that you have missed one or more transitions.

170. Question "Miracle" States

A miracle state is one that has transitions out of it but none into it, something that should be true only of start points. This is also an indication that you have missed one or more transitions.

8.3 Substate Modeling Guidelines

171. Model Substates for Targeted Complexity

The UML state chart diagram presented in Figure 28 is not complete because it does not model any postenrollment states of a *Seminar*. Figure 29 models the entire life cycle of a *Seminar*, depicting Figure 28 as a collection of substates of a new *Enrollment* composite state, also called a superstate. Normally, you would include labels on the transitions, as they are modeled in Figure 28, but they were omitted from Figure 29 for the sake of simplicity. Modeling substates makes sense when an existing state exhibits complex behavior, thereby motivating you to explore its substates. Introducing a superstate makes sense when several existing states share a common entry or exit condition (Douglass 1999). In Figure 28 you can see that all of the states share a common *closed* transition to the final state.

172. Aggregate Common Substate Transitions

In Figure 29, you can see that the *cancelled* transition is depicted as leaving the *Enrollment* superstate, but to simplify the diagram, not every single substate is depicted as in Figure 28. Had the substates all shared an entry transition, or another exit transition, the same approach would have been taken for those transitions, too. The guards and actions, if any, on the transitions being aggregated must be identical.

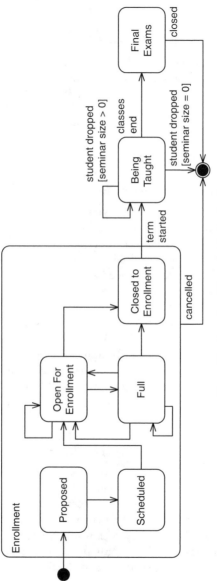

Figure 29. Complete life cycle of a seminar.

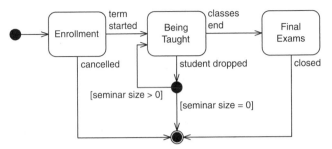

Figure 30. Top-level state chart for seminar.

173. Create a Hierarchy of State Charts for Very Complex Entities

Although showing substates in this manner works well, the resulting diagrams can become quite complex—just imagine what would happen to Figure 29 if the *Being Taught* state also had substates. An alternative approach would be to create a hierarchy of UML state chart diagrams; for example, Figure 30 represents the top-level view and Figure 28 depicts a more detailed view. The advantage of this approach is that another detailed diagram could be developed to explore the *Being Taught* state as required.

174. Always Include Initial and Final States on Top-Level State Charts

A top-level UML state chart, such as the one depicted in Figure 29, should represent the entire life cycle of an entity, including its "birth" and eventual "death." Lower-level diagrams may not always include initial and final states, particularly diagrams that model the "middle states" of an entity's life cycle.

8.4 Transition and Action Guidelines

A transition is a progression from one state to another and will be triggered by an event that is either internal or external to the entity being modeled. For a class, transitions are typically the result of the invocation of an operation that causes an important change in state, although not all method invocations will result in transitions. An action is something—in the case of a class, it is an operation—that is invoked by/on the entity being modeled.

175. Name Software Actions Using Implementation-Language Naming Conventions

The actions in Figure 28 follow the Java naming convention for operations (Vermeulen et al. 2000) because the intention is to implement this system using Java. Had another language been our target, we would have followed the appropriate naming conventions.

176. Name Actor Actions Using Prose

UML state chart diagrams can be used to model the life cycle of nonsoftware entities, in particular, actors on UML use case diagrams. For example, the *Student* actor likely has states such as *Accepted, Full Time, Part Time, Graduated, Masters, Doctoral,* and *Postdoctoral,* exhibiting different behaviors in each one. When you are modeling the real-world actor, as opposed to the software class *Student,* the transitions between these states would be better worded using prose such as *drop seminar* and *pay fees* instead of *dropSeminar()* and *payFees(),* because people in the real world do things—they don't execute operations.

177. Indicate Entry Actions Only When Applicable for All Entry Transitions

In Figure 28, you can see that, upon entry into the *Closed To Enrollment* state, the operation *notifyInstructor()* is invoked via the *entry/* action label. The implication is that this operation will be invoked every single time that this state is entered. If you don't want this to occur, then associate actions with specific entry transitions. For example, the *addStudent()* action is taken on the *student enrolled* transition to *Open For Enrollment* but not to the *opened* transition. This is because you don't always add a student each time you enter this state.

178. Indicate Exit Actions Only When Applicable for All Exit Transitions

Exit actions, indicated with the *exit/* label, work in a manner similar to entry actions.

179. Model Recursive Transitions Only When You Want to Exit and Reenter the State

A recursive transition, also called a "mouse-ear" transition, is one that has the same state for both of its end points. An important implication is that the entity is exiting and then reentering the state. Therefore, any operations that would be invoked due to *entry/* or *exit/* action labels would be automatically invoked. This would be the case with the recursive transitions of the *Open For Enrollment* state of Figure 28, where the current seminar size is logged on entry.

180. Name Transition Events in Past Tense

The transition events in Figure 28, such as *seminar split* and *cancelled*, are written in past tense to reflect the fact that the transitions are the results of events. That is, an event occurs before a transition, and thus it should be referred to in past tense.

181. Place Transition Labels Near the Source State

Although Figure 28 is complex, wherever possible the transition labels, such as *seminar split* and *student enrolled*, were placed as close to the source as possible. Furthermore, the labels were justified (left and right, respectively) so that they are visually close to the source state.

182. Place Transitions Labels on the Basis of Transition Direction

To make it easier to identify which label goes with a transition, place transition labels according to the following heuristics:

- above-transition lines going left to right,
- below-transition lines going right to left,
- right-of-transition lines going down,
- left-of-transition lines going up.

8.5 Guard Guidelines

A guard is a condition that must be true in order to traverse a transition.

183. Do Not Overlap Guards

The guards on similar transitions leaving a state must be consistent with one another. For example, guards such as $x < 0$, $x = 0$, and $x > 0$ are consistent, whereas guards such as $x <= 0$ and $x >= 0$ are not consistent because they overlap. (It isn't clear what should happen when x is 0.) In Figure 29, the guards on the *student dropped* transitions from the *Being Taught* state do not overlap.

184. Introduce Junctions to Visually Localize Guards

In Figure 29, there are two transitions from *Being Taught* as the result of the *student dropped* event, whereas there is only one in Figure 30—the transitions are combined into a single one that leads to a junction point (the filled circle). The advantage of this approach is that the two guards are now depicted close to one another on the diagram, making it easier to determine that the guards don't overlap.

185. Use Guards Even if They Do Not Form a Complete Set

It is possible that the guards on the transitions from a state will not form a complete set. For example, a bank account object might transition from the *Open* state to the *Needs Authorization* state when a large deposit is made to it. However, a deposit transition with a "small deposit" guard may not be modeled—you're following the AM *Depict Models Simply* practice and only including pertinent information—although it would be implied.

186. *Never Place a Guard on an Initial Transition*

Douglass (1999) says it best: What does the object do when the guard evaluates to false?

187. *Use Consistent Language Naming Guards*

Figure 28 includes guards such as *seat available* and *no seat available*, which are consistently worded. However, had the various guards been worded *seats left, no seat left, no seats left, no seats available, seat unavailable*, they would have been inconsistent and harder to understand.

9.

UML Activity

Diagrams

UML activity diagrams are the object-oriented equivalent of flow charts and data-flow diagrams from structured development (Gane and Sarson 1979). In UML 1.x, UML activity diagrams were a specialization of UML state chart diagrams, although in UML 2.x they are full-fledged artifacts. UML activity diagrams are used to explore the logic of

- a complex operation,
- a complex business rule,
- a single use case,
- several use cases,
- a business process, and
- software processes.

9.1 General Guidelines

188. *Place the Start Point in the Top-Left Corner*

A start point is modeled with a filled circle, using the same notation that UML state chart diagrams use. Every UML activity diagram should have a starting point, and placing it at the top-left corner reflects the way that people in Western cultures begin reading. Figure 31, depicting the business process of enrolling in a university, takes this approach.

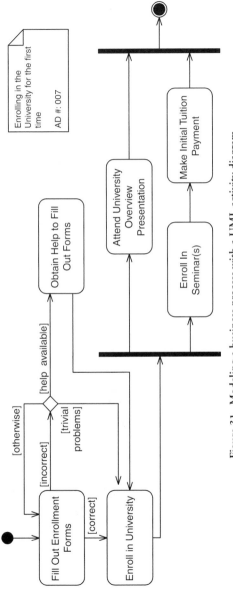

Enrolling in the
University for the first
time

AD #: 007

Figure 31. Modeling a business process with a UML activity diagram.

93

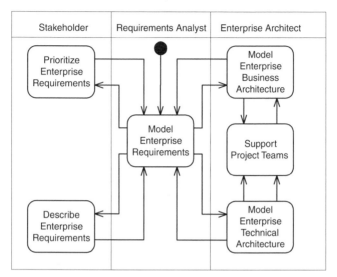

Figure 32. UML activity diagram for the enterprise architectural modeling (simplified).

189. Include an Ending Point

An ending point is modeled with a filled circle with a border around it. Fowler and Scott's (1999) style is to make ending points optional—sometimes an activity is simply a dead end—but if this is the case, then there is no harm in indicating that the only transition is to an ending point. That way, when someone else reads your diagram, they know that you have considered how to exit these activities.

Sometimes, however, the guidelines don't apply. Figure 32 does not include an ending point because it describes a continuous process.

190. Simplify Operations Requiring Flow Charts

If an operation is so complex that you need to develop a UML activity diagram to understand it, then you should consider refactoring it.

9.2 Activity Guidelines

An activity on a UML activity diagram typically represents the invocation of an operation, a step in a business process, or an entire business process.

191. Question "Black-Hole" Activities

A black-hole activity is one that has transitions into it but none out of it, typically indicating that you have missed one or more transitions.

192. Question "Miracle" Activities

A miracle activity is one that has transitions out of it but none into it, something that should be true only of starting points. Once again, this is an indication that you have missed one or more transitions.

9.3 Decision-Point Guidelines

A decision point is modeled as a diamond on a UML activity diagram.

193. Reflect the Previous Activity by Using Decision Points

In Figure 31, you can see that there is no label on the decision point, unlike traditional flow charts, which would include text describing the actual decision being made. You need to imply that the decision concerns whether the person was enrolled in the university based on the activity that the decision point follows. The guards, depicted using the format [*description*], on the transitions leaving the decision point also help to describe the decision point.

194. Avoid Superfluous Decision Points

The *Fill Out Enrollment Forms* activity in Figure 31 includes an implied decision point, a check to see that the forms are filled out properly. This simplified the diagram by avoiding an additional diamond.

9.4 Guard Guidelines

A guard is a condition that must be true in order to traverse a transition.

195. Ensure That Each Transition Leaving a Decision Point Has a Guard

This ensures that you have thought through all possibilities for that decision point.

196. Do Not Overlap Guards

The guards on the transitions leaving a decision point, or an activity, must be consistent with one another. For example, guards such as $x < 0$, $x = 0$, and $x > 0$ are consistent, whereas guards such as $x <= 0$ and $x >= 0$ are not consistent because they overlap. (It isn't clear what should happen when x is 0.) In Figure 31, the guards on the exit transitions from the *Fill Out Enrollment Forms* activity do not overlap, nor do the guards on the decision point.

197. Ensure That Guards on Decision Points Form a Complete Set

It must always be possible to leave a decision point. Therefore, the guards on its exit transitions must be complete. For example, guards such as $x < 0$ and $x > 0$ are not complete because it isn't clear what happens when x is 0.

198. Ensure That Exit Transition Guards and Activity Invariants Form a Complete Set

An activity invariant is a condition that is always true when your system is processing an activity. For example, in Figure 31 an invariant of the *Enroll In University* activity is that the person is not yet officially a student. Clearly, the conditions that are true while processing an activity must not overlap with its exit conditions. Furthermore, the invariants and exit conditions must form a complete set. In other words, the conditions that define when you are in an activity plus the conditions that define when you leave the activity must add up.

199. Apply an [Otherwise] Guard for "Fall-Through" Logic

In Figure 31, you can see that one of the transitions on the decision point is labeled *Otherwise*, a catchall condition for the situation in which problems with the forms are not trivial and help is not available. This avoided a very wordy guard, thus simplifying the diagram.

200. Model Guards Only if They Add Value

A transition will not necessarily include a guard, even when an activity includes several exit transitions. When a UML activity diagram is used to model a software process (Figure 32) or a business process (Figure 33), the transitions often represent sharing or movement of information and objects between activities, a situation in which guards often make less sense. Follow Agile Modeling's (AM) (Chapter 12) principle of *Depict Models Simply* and only indicate a guard on a transition if it adds value.

9.5 Parallel-Activity Guidelines

It is possible to show that activities can occur in parallel, depicted in Figure 31 by two parallel bars. The first bar is called a fork: it has one transition entering it and two or more transitions leaving it. The second bar is a join, with two or more transitions entering it and only one leaving it.

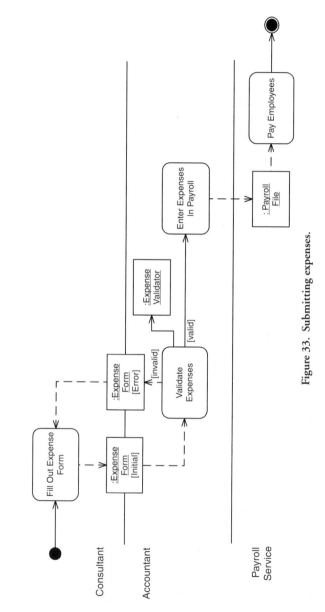

Figure 33. Submitting expenses.

201. Ensure That Forks Have Corresponding Joins

In Figure 31, you can see that the business process forks into two parallel streams, one where the person attends a presentation and another where he or she signs up and pays for courses. The process forks—the person performs these activities—and when both streams are complete, the process continues from there (in this case it simply ends). In general, for every start (fork), there is an end (join).

202. Ensure That a Fork Has Only One Entry Transition

When you find that you want to have several transitions into the same fork, you should first merge them by having them enter a single diamond and then have a single transition from the diamond into the fork. However, this situation is also a good indication that you've either missed an activity, likely where the merge occurs, or that you really don't have parallel activities at this point.

203. Ensure That a Join Has Only One Exit Transition

The desire to have several exit transitions is a good indication that you still have parallel activities occurring; therefore, move your join further along in the overall process.

204. Avoid Superfluous Forks

Figure 32 depicts a simplified description of the software process of enterprise architectural modeling, a part of the *Infrastructure Management* discipline of the Enterprise Unified Process (EUP)[4]. There is a significant opportunity for parallelism in this process. In fact, all of these activities could happen in parallel, but forks were not introduced because they would only have cluttered the diagram.

---

[4] Visit www.ronin-intl.com/publications/unifiedProcess.html for details.

9.6 Swimlane Guidelines

A swimlane is a way to group activities performed by the same actor on an activity diagram or to group activities in a single thread (Douglass 1999).

205. Order Swimlanes in a Logical Manner

Although there are no semantics behind the ordering of swimlanes, there often is a natural ordering for them. For example, in Figure 32 you can see that the swimlanes are listed left to right in the relative order that the activities would occur in a serial process (even though this one is iterative)—stakeholders will start by identifying and prioritizing requirements, the analyst will model them, then the architects will act on them.

206. Apply Swimlanes to Linear Processes

Swimlanes are best applied to linear processes, unlike the one depicted in Figure 32, where the logic proceeds from one activity to another. The steps that customers take to check an order out of a grocery store are a perfect example of a relatively linear process. A diagram for that activity would likely include three swimlanes, one for the customer, one for the checkout clerk, and one for the person who bags the groceries.

207. Have Less Than Five Swimlanes

A disadvantage of swimlanes is that they reduce your freedom to arrange activities in a space-effective manner, often increasing the size of your diagrams. When a diagram has a small number of swimlanes, there is less chance that this problem will occur.

208. Consider Swimareas for Complex Diagrams

When you need several swimlanes—for example, if Figure 32 were to include all of the activities of the Infrastructure Management discipline, it would include swimlanes for roles such as Reuse Manager, Program Manager, Software Process Manager, and Human Resource Manager—you would discover that the swimlanes would force you to arrange the activities in a non-optimal way (the transitions between some activities would cross the page). Another approach would be to use swimareas, sections of related activities, instead of a formal swimlane. Fowler and Scott (1999) call these swimareas "nonlinear zones."

209. Reorganize into Smaller Activity Diagrams When Swimareas Include Several Activities

When a swimarea includes several activities, you may instead decide to introduce a UML package, or simply a higher-level activity, which is then described by a detailed UML activity diagram. For example, Figure 32 may simply be the detailed description of a *Model the Enterprise* activity on a high-level diagram for that EUP discipline.

210. Consider Horizontal Swimlanes for Business Processes

In Figure 33 the swimlanes are drawn horizontally, going against common convention of drawing them vertically. Because project stakeholders in Western cultures typically read from left to right, this helps to increase the understandability of a UML activity diagram used to depict business processes. Also notice how the outside borders of the swimlanes have been dropped to simplify the diagram.

211. Model the Key Activities in the Primary Swimlane

The primary swimlane is the left-most swimlane on vertical activity diagrams and the top swimlane on horizontal diagrams, and this is where Evitts (2000) suggests that you put the key activities of UML activity diagrams. For example, when using a UML activity diagram to model the logic of a use case, an effective approach is to depict the basic course of action, also known as the happy path (Ambler 2001), in the primary swimlane.

9.7 Action-Object Guidelines

Activities act on objects. In the strict object-oriented sense of the term, an action object is a system object, a software construct. In the looser sense, and much more useful for business application modeling, an action object is any sort of item. For example, in Figure 33 the *ExpenseForm* action object is likely a paper form.

212. Place Shared Action Objects on Swimlane Separators

In Figure 33, you can see that the *ExpenseForm* action object is placed on the line separator between the *Consultant* and *Accountant* swimlanes. This was done because the *ExpenseForm* is critical to both swimlanes and because it is manipulated in both, very likely being something on which the two people will work together (at least when there is a problem).

213. Apply State Names When an Object Appears Several Times

The *ExpenseForm* object appears twice on the diagram—an initial version of it and one with errors. To distinguish between them, their state names—in this case *Initial* and *Error*—are indicated using the same notation as for guards on transitions. This notation may be applied to any object on any UML diagram, including UML sequence diagrams and UML collaboration diagrams.

214. Reflect the Life-Cycle Stage of an Action Object in Its State Name

You depict the same action object on a UML activity diagram in several places because it is pertinent to what is being modeled and because the object itself has changed (it has progressed through one or more stages of its life cycle).

215. *Show Only Critical Inputs and Outputs*

Although Figure 33 shows *ExpenseForm* as an output of the *Fill Out Expense Form* activity, you know it's an output because the transition is depicted using a dashed arrow. However, there isn't a lot of value in doing so because it's clear that an expense form would be the output of that activity. Remember AM's practice *Depict Models Simply* and only model something if it adds value.

216. *Depict Action Objects as Smaller Than Activities*

The focus of a UML activity diagram is activities, not the actions implementing or being produced by those activities. Therefore, you can show this focus by having larger activity symbols. To depict the fact that an activity is implemented by an action object, you use a solid arrow. In Figure 33 the *ExpenseValidator* object implements the *Validate Expenses* activity.

10.

UML Component

Diagrams

UML component diagrams show the dependencies among software components, including the classifiers that specify them, such as implementation classes; and the artifacts that implement them; such as source-code files, binary-code files, executable files, scripts, and tables. Create them to

- model the low-level design configuration of your system,
- model the technical infrastructure (Ambler 1998), or
- model the business/domain architecture for your organization (Ambler 1998).

10.1 Component Guidelines

In Figure 34, components are modeled as rectangles with two smaller rectangles jutting out from the left-hand side. Components realize one or more interfaces, modeled using the lollipop notation in Figure 34, and may have dependencies on other components or interfaces. As you can see, the *Persistence* component has a dependency on the *Corporate DB* component.

217. Apply Descriptive Names
to Architectural Components

Architectural diagrams are often viewed by a wide range of people who may not be familiar with your project. Therefore,

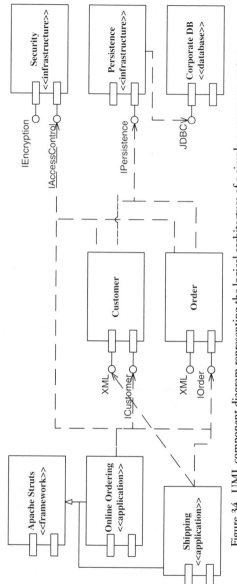

Figure 34. UML component diagram representing the logical architecture of a simple e-commerce system.

component names need to be understandable. For example, most of the components in Figure 34, with the exception of *Corporate DB*, are named using full words such as *Customer* and *Persistence*. The name *Corporate DB* was used over *Corporate Database* because that is what it is known as within the company—abbreviations are preferable only when they are in common use.

218. Apply Environment-Specific Naming Conventions to Detailed Design Components

When you are creating a detailed component model, perhaps to understand the physical configuration of your system, then name your components using environment-specific names. For example, a Java source-code file would be named *Customer.java*, a Windows library would be named *auditLogger.dll*, and a document would be named *User Manual.doc*.

219. Apply Consistent Textual Stereotypes

Table 6 summarizes common stereotypes that you may want to consider applying to components on UML component diagrams.

220. Avoid Modeling Data and User Interface Components

UML component diagrams can be used to model various aspects of your detailed design. Because the UML does not yet address user interface or database modeling, many developers will often try to model these aspects of their system using component diagrams. Don't do this. Component diagrams really aren't well suited for these tasks. I personally suggest using modified collaboration diagrams for user interface modeling (Ambler 2001), and other methodologists suggest modifications on state charts (Larman 2002) or activity diagrams (Schneider and Winters 2001) and most prefer modified class diagrams for data modeling. My advice is to follow AM's

Table 6. Common Stereotypes.

Stereotype	Indicates
<<application>>	A "front end" of your system, such as the collection of HTML pages and ASP/JSPs that work with them for a browser-based system or the collection of screens and controller classes for a GUI-based system.
<<database>>	A hierarchical, relational, object-relational, network, or object-oriented database.
<<document>>	A printed or electronic document.
<<executable>>	A software component that can be executed on a node.
<<file>>	A data file.
<<infrastructure>>	A technical component within your system, such as a persistence service or an audit logger.
<<library>>	An object or function library.
<<source code>>	A source-code file, such as a *.java file or a *.cpp file.
<<table>>	A data table within a database.
<<web service>>	One or more Web services.
<<XML DTD>>	An XML DTD.

(Chapter 12) practice of *Apply the Right Artifact(s)* and pick the right artifact for the job. In these cases, a UML component diagram isn't it.

10.2 Interface Guidelines

An interface is a collection of operation signatures and/or attribute definitions that ideally defines a cohesive set of behaviors. Interfaces are implemented, "realized" in UML parlance, by classes and components; to realize an interface, a class or component must implement the operations and attributes defined by the interface. Any given class or component may implement zero or more interfaces, and one or more classes or components can implement the same interface.

221. Prefer Lollipop Notation to Depict Interfaces Realized by Components

There are two ways to indicate that a class or component implements an interface: the lollipop notation used in Figure 34 or a realization association (a dashed line with a closed arrowhead) as in Figure 35 with the *IStudent* interface. The lollipop notation is preferred because it is visually compact; the class box and realization line approach tends to clutter your diagrams.

222. Prefer the Left-Hand Side of a Component for Interface Lollipops

Although you can put an interface lollipop on any side of a component, the SQL interface is depicted on the right-hand side of *TStudent* in Figure 35. The most common approach, however, is to place them on the left to increase the consistency within your component diagrams.

223. Show Only Relevant Interfaces

AM's practice *Depict Models Simply* advises that you keep your diagrams as simple as possible, and one way to do that is to depict only the interfaces that are applicable to the goals of your diagram. For example, in Figure 34 you can see that the *XML* interface is modeled for the *Order* component but it is not being used, indicating that you might not want to depict it at this time. However, if one of the goals of your model is to show that all of your business/domain components implement this common interface, presumably so that every component has a standard way to get at the data structures that they support, then it makes sense to show it. In short, don't clutter your diagrams with extraneous information.

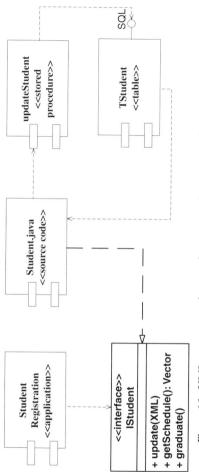

Figure 35. UML component diagram for some student aspects of a university system.

10.3 Dependency and Inheritance Guidelines

Components will have dependencies either on other components or, better yet, on the interfaces of other components. As you can see in Figure 34 and Figure 35, dependencies are modeled using a dashed line with an open arrowhead.

224. Model Dependencies from Left to Right

You should strive to arrange your components so that you can draw dependencies from left to right. This increases the consistency of your diagrams and helps you to identify potential circular dependencies in your design. For example, a circular dependency exists in Figure 35: *Student.Java* depends on *updateStudent*, which depends on *TStudent*, which in turn depends on *Student.Java*. This was easy to detect because the dependence from *TStudent* to *Student.Java* went from right to left, whereas all others went in the opposite direction.

Note that if your diagram is layered vertically, then you will want to model dependencies top to bottom.

225. Place Inheriting Components Below Base Components

Inheritance between components is possible—in this case between *Shipping* and *Apache Struts* in Figure 34—and, as you can see, the inheriting component is shown below the parent component.

226. Make Components Dependent Only on Interfaces

By making components dependent on the interfaces of other components instead of on the other components themselves, you make it possible to replace the component without having to rewrite the components that depend on it. For example, in Figure 34 the *Customer* and *Order* components both depend on the interface to the *Persistence* component to store them in the database. Perhaps the first implementation of this component was developed in-house, but because you quickly found out how complicated persistence could be (Ambler 2001), you decided to purchase a persistence framework. To swap this persistence framework into place, you merely need to implement the same interface for it, in the case *IPersistence.* Had your domain components relied on the actual implementation of your "Persistence" component, instead of its interface, you would have needed to rewrite portions of your domain components to use its new implementation.

227. *Avoid Modeling Compilation Dependencies*

Although it is possible to model compilation dependencies in UML component diagrams, there are better ways to record this information, such as in the build/compile scripts for your application. A good rule of thumb is that if you're showing compilation dependencies on your component diagrams, then you've likely overmodeled your system. Step back and ask yourself if this information is actually adding value to your diagram(s).

11.

UML Deployment

Diagrams

A UML deployment diagram depicts a static view of the run-time configuration of hardware nodes and the software components that run on those nodes. UML deployment diagrams show the hardware for your system, the software that is installed on that hardware, and the middleware used to connect the disparate machines to one another. You create a UML deployment model to

- explore the issues involved in installing your system into production,
- explore the dependencies that your system has with other systems that are currently in, or planned for, your production environment,
- depict a major deployment configuration of a business application,
- design the hardware and software configuration of an embedded system, or
- depict the hardware/network infrastructure of an organization.

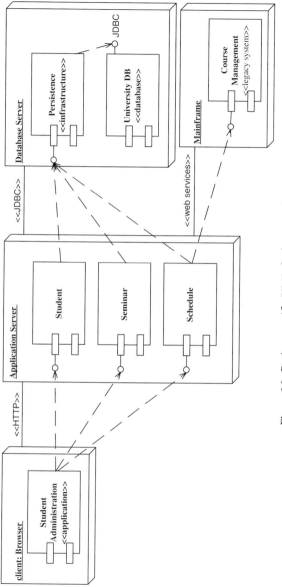

Figure 36. Project-specific UML deployment diagram.

113

11.1 General Guidelines

228. Indicate Software Components on Project-Specific Diagrams

Figure 36 depicts a UML deployment diagram for a university administration system. This diagram depicts how the major software components that comprise a single application are to be deployed into the production environment, enabling the project team to identify its deployment strategy.

229. Focus on Nodes and Communication Associations on Enterprise-Level Diagrams

Figure 37 is an example of a style of UML deployment diagram (applying visual stereotypes) often referred to as a network diagram or technical architecture diagram, depicting the technical infrastructure of a simple organization. Figure 37 is a very simple example; many organizations would have tens if not hundreds of nodes on such a diagram.

Although indicating the deployment of components can be useful on diagrams of limited scope, such as Figure 36, it can quickly become cumbersome. The focus of Figure 37 is high level, that of the enterprise, and therefore, the minute details of which software components are deployed to which hardware nodes do not need to be shown. You may choose to capture this information in your CASE tool, but that doesn't imply that you need to show it on your diagram.

230. Group Common Nodes

Evitts (2000) suggests that you group nodes that share common responsibilities, or that share a common location, to visually associate them.

11.2 Node and Component Guidelines

A node, depicted as a three-dimensional box, represents a computational unit, typically a single piece of hardware, such as

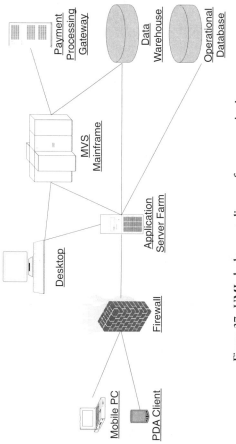

Figure 37. UML deployment diagram for an organization.

a computer, network router, mainframe, sensor, or personal digital assistant. Components, depicted as rectangles with two smaller rectangles jutting out from the left-hand side (the same notation used on UML component diagrams), represent software artifacts such as files, frameworks, or reusable domain functionality.

231. Use Descriptive Terms to Name Nodes

In Figure 36, you can see that the nodes have names such as *client*, *Application Server*, *Database Server*, and *Mainframe*. All of these terms would be instantly recognizable to the developers within this organization because those are the terms they use on a daily basis. Keep it simple.

232. Model Only Vital Software Components

Although Figure 36 includes software components, it does not depict every single one. For example, the client machine very likely has other software components installed on it, such as the operating system and application software, but those components are not shown because they are not relevant. The reality is that each node may have tens if not hundreds of software components deployed to it. Your goal isn't to depict all of them; it is merely to depict those components that are vital to the understanding of your system. If you need to explore the relationships between software components, you should create a UML component diagram instead, effectively following the Agile Modeling's (AM) (Chapter 12) practice of *Apply the Right Artifact(s)*.

233. Apply Consistent Stereotypes to Components

Apply the same stereotypes to components on UML deployment diagrams that you would apply on UML component diagrams.

234. Apply Visual Stereotypes to Nodes

Figure 37 depicts nodes using visual stereotypes. For example, the mobile PC is shown as a laptop and the databases are shown using traditional database drum notation. There are few standards for applying visual stereotypes on UML deployment diagrams, but the general rule of thumb is to use the most appropriate clip art that you can find. Figure 37 was drawn using Microsoft Visio, a drawing package that comes with a large selection of network diagramming stencils that are ideal for UML deployment models.

11.3 Dependency and Communication-Association Guidelines

Communication associations, often called connections, are depicted as lines connecting nodes. Dependencies between

Table 7. Common Stereotypes for Communication Associations.

Stereotype	Implication
asynchronous	An asynchronous connection, perhaps via a message bus or message queue.
HTTP	HyperText Transport Protocol, an Internet protocol.
JDBC	Java Database Connectivity, a Java API for database access.
ODBC	Open Database Connectivity, a Microsoft API for database access.
RMI	Remote Method Invocation, a Java communication protocol.
RPC	Communication via remote procedure calls.
synchronous	A synchronous connect where the sender waits for a response from the receiver.
web services	Communication is via Web services protocols such as SOAP and UDDI.

components are modeled as dashed arrows, the same notation used on other UML diagrams.

235. Indicate Communication Protocols Via Stereotypes

Communication associations support one or more communication protocols, each of which should be indicated by a UML stereotype. In Figure 36, you can see that the HTTP, JDBC, and Web services protocols are indicated using this approach. Table 7 provides a representative list of stereotypes for communication associations, but your organization will want to develop its own specific standards.

236. Model Only Critical Dependencies Between Components

In Figure 36 the dependencies between the domain components deployed to the application server are not modeled because they weren't pertinent to the diagram (and they would be better modeled in greater detail on a UML component diagram). However, the dependency between the components on the database server was modeled because it helped to show that database access by domain components isn't direct; they instead need to go through the persistence framework—a common architecture best practice (Ambler 2001). Follow the AM practice *Depict Models Simply* and only model information that is pertinent to the task at hand.

12.

Agile Modeling

Agile Modeling (AM) (Ambler 2002) is a chaordic (Hock 2000), practice-based methodology for effective modeling of software-based systems. The AM methodology is a collection of practices, guided by principles and values that can be applied by software professionals on a day-to-day basis. AM is not a prescriptive process. It does not define detailed procedures for how to create a given type of model, but it does provide advice for how to be effective as a modeler. It's "touchy-feely," not hard and fast—think of AM as an art, not a science.

12.1 Values

The foundation of AM is its five values, the first four adopted from eXtreme Programming (XP) (Beck 2000):

- communication,
- courage,
- feedback,
- simplicity, and
- humility.

12.2 Principles

The principles of AM, which are based on its values, define the basis for its practices. The principles are organized into two collections: the core principles, which you must fully adopt to be able to claim you are "agile modeling," and the

Table 8. Principles of AM.

Core	Supplementary
■ Assume Simplicity ■ Embrace Change ■ Enabling the Next Effort Is Your Secondary Goal ■ Incremental Change ■ Maximize Stakeholder Investment ■ Model with a Purpose ■ Multiple Models ■ Quality Work ■ Rapid Feedback ■ Software Is Your Primary Goal ■ Travel Light	■ Content Is More Important Than Representation ■ Everyone Can Learn from Everyone Else ■ Know Your Models ■ Know Your Tools ■ Local Adaptation ■ Open and Honest Communication ■ Work with People's Instincts

Table 9. Practices of AM.

Core	Supplementary
■ Active Stakeholder Participation ■ Apply the Right Artifact(s) ■ Collective Ownership ■ Consider Testability ■ Create Several Models in Parallel ■ Create Simple Content ■ Depict Models Simply ■ Display Models Publicly ■ Iterate to Another Artifact ■ Model in Small Increments ■ Model with Others ■ Prove It with Code ■ Use the Simplest Tools	■ Apply Modeling Standards ■ Apply Patterns Gently ■ Discard Temporary Models ■ Formalize Contract Models ■ Model to Communicate ■ Model to Understand ■ Reuse Existing Resources ■ Update Only When It Hurts

supplementary principles, which support the core. Table 8 lists the principles of AM.

12.3 Practices

The practices of AM define effective techniques for modeling. As with the principles, the practices are organized into two groups, core and supplementary. Table 9 lists the practices of AM.

Summary

General Guidelines

1. *Avoid crossing lines.*
2. *Depict crossing lines as a jump.*
3. *Avoid diagonal or curved lines.*
4. *Apply consistently sized symbols.*
5. *Arrange symbols symmetrically.*
6. *Include white space in diagrams.*
7. *Organize diagrams left to right, top to bottom.*
8. *Show only what you have to show.*
9. *Prefer well-known notation over esoteric notation.*
10. *Reorganize large diagrams into several smaller ones.*
11. *Prefer single-page diagrams.*
12. *Focus on content first, appearance second.*
13. *Describe diagrams with a note.*
14. *Set a convention for placement of diagram legends.*
15. *Apply consistent, readable fonts.*
16. *Set and follow effective naming conventions.*
17. *Apply common domain terminology in names.*
18. *Apply language naming conventions on design diagrams.*
19. *Name common elements consistently across diagrams.*
20. *Indicate unknowns with a question mark.*

21. *Consider applying color to your diagrams.*

22. *Apply color or different fonts sparingly.*

23. *Left-justify text in notes.*

24. *Name stereotypes in* <<user interface>> *and* <<UI>> *format.*

25. *Prefer naming conventions over stereotypes.*

26. *Introduce new stereotypes sparingly.*

27. *Apply stereotypes consistently.*

28. *Prefer notes over OCL or ASL to indicate constraints.*

29. *Begin use case names with a strong verb.*

UML Use Case Diagram Guidelines

30. *Name use cases using domain terminology.*

31. *Imply timing considerations by stacking use cases.*

32. *Place your primary actor(s) in the top-left corner of the diagram.*

33. *Draw actors on the outside edges of a use case diagram.*

34. *Name actors with singular, domain-relevant nouns.*

35. *Associate each actor with one or more use cases.*

36. *Name actors to model roles, not job titles.*

37. *Use* <<system>> *to indicate system actors.*

38. *Don't allow actors to interact with one another.*

39. *Introduce an actor called "time" to initiate scheduled events.*

40. *Indicate an association between an actor and a use case if the actor appears within the use case logic.*

41. *Avoid arrowheads on actor-use case relationships.*

42. *Apply* <<include>> *when you know exactly when to invoke the use case.*

43. *Apply* <<extend>> *when a use case may be invoked across several use case steps.*

44. *Apply* <<extend>> *associations sparingly.*

45. *Generalize use cases when a single condition results in significantly new business logic.*

46. *Do not apply* <<uses>>, <<includes>>, *or* <<extends>>.

47. *Avoid more than two levels of use case associations.*

48. *Place an included use case to the right of the invoking use case.*

49. *Place an extending use case below the parent use case.*

50. *Apply the "is like" rule to use case generalization.*

51. *Place an inheriting use case below the base use case.*

52. *Apply the "is like" rule to actor inheritance.*

53. *Place an inheriting actor below the parent actor.*

54. *Indicate release scope with a system boundary box.*

55. *Avoid meaningless system boundary boxes.*

UML Class Diagram Guidelines

56. *Identify responsibilities on domain class models.*

57. *Indicate visibility only on design models.*

58. *Indicate language-dependent visibility with property strings.*

59. *Indicate types on analysis models only when the type is an actual requirement.*

60. *Be consistent with attribute names and types.*

61. *Model association classes on analysis diagrams.*

62. *Do not name associations that have association classes.*

63. *Center the dashed line of an association class.*

64. *Use common terminology for class names.*

65. *Prefer complete singular nouns for class names.*

66. *Name operations with a strong verb.*

67. *Name attributes with a domain-based noun.*

68. *Do not model scaffolding code.*

69. *Do not model keys.*

70. *Never show classes with just two compartments.*

71. *Label uncommon class compartments.*

72. *Include an ellipsis (. . .) at the end of incomplete lists.*

73. *List static operations/attributes before instance operations/attributes.*

74. *List operations/attributes in decreasing visibility.*

75. *For parameters that are objects, list only their type.*

76. *Develop consistent operation and attribute signatures.*

77. *Avoid stereotypes implied by language naming conventions.*

78. *Indicate exceptions in an operation's property string.*

79. *Reflect implementation language constraints in interface definitions.*

80. *Name interfaces according to language naming conventions.*

81. *Prefer "lollipop" notation to indicate realization of an interface.*

82. *Define interfaces separately from your classes.*

83. *Do not model the operations and attributes of interfaces in your classes.*

84. *Model relationships horizontally.*

85. *Model collaboration between two elements only when they have a relationship.*

86. *Model a dependency when the relationship is transitory.*

87. *Tree-rout similar relationships to a common class.*

88. *Always indicate the multiplicity.*

89. *Avoid a multiplicity of "*".*

90. *Replace relationship lines with attribute types.*

91. *Do not model implied relationships.*

92. *Do not model every dependency.*

93. *Center names on associations.*

94. *Write concise association names in active voice.*

95. *Indicate directionality to clarify an association name.*

96. *Name unidirectional associations in the same direction.*

97. *Word association names left to right.*

98. *Indicate role names when multiple associations between two classes exist.*

99. *Indicate role names on recursive associations.*

100. *Make associations bi-directional only when collaboration occurs in both directions.*

101. *Redraw inherited associations only when something changes.*

102. *Question multiplicities involving minimums and maximums.*

103. *Apply the sentence rule for inheritance.*

104. *Place subclasses below superclasses.*

105. *Beware of data-based inheritance.*

106. *A subclass should inherit everything.*

107. *Apply the sentence rule for aggregation.*

108. *Be interested in both the whole and the part.*
109. *Place the whole to the left of the part.*
110. *Apply composition to aggregates of physical items.*
111. *Apply composition when the parts share their persistence life cycle with the whole.*
112. *Don't worry about the diamonds.*

Package Diagram Guidelines

113. *Create class package diagrams to logically organize your design.*
114. *Create UML component diagrams to physically organize your design.*
115. *Place inheriting packages below base packages.*
116. *Vertically layer class package diagrams.*
117. *Create use case package diagrams to organize your requirements.*
118. *Include actors on use case package diagrams.*
119. *Horizontally arrange use case package diagrams.*
120. *Give packages simple, descriptive names.*
121. *Make packages cohesive.*
122. *Indicate architectural layers with stereotypes on packages.*
123. *Avoid cyclic dependencies between packages.*
124. *Reflect internal relationships in package dependencies.*

UML Sequence Diagram Guidelines

125. *Strive for left-to-right ordering of messages.*
126. *Layer classifiers.*

127. *Give an actor the same name as a class, if necessary.*

128. *Include a prose description of the logic.*

129. *Place proactive system actors on the left-most side of your diagram.*

130. *Place reactive system actors on the right-most side of your diagram.*

131. *Avoid modeling object destruction.*

132. *Don't sweat activation boxes.*

133. *Name objects when you reference them in messages.*

134. *Name objects when several of the same type exist.*

135. *Apply textual stereotypes to classifiers consistently.*

136. *Apply visual stereotypes sparingly.*

137. *Focus on critical interactions.*

138. *Justify message names beside the arrowhead.*

139. *Create objects directly.*

140. *Apply operation signatures for software messages.*

141. *Apply prose for messages involving human and organization actors.*

142. *Prefer names over types for parameters.*

143. *Indicate types as parameter placeholders.*

144. *Apply the* <<include>> *stereotype for use case invocations.*

145. *Do not model obvious return values.*

146. *Model a return value only when you need to refer to it elsewhere on a diagram.*

147. *Justify return values beside the arrowhead.*

148. *Model return values as part of a method invocation.*

149. *Indicate types as return-value placeholders.*

150. *Indicate the actual value for simple return values.*

UML Collaboration Diagram Guidelines

151. *Create instance-level diagrams to explore object design issues.*

152. *Create specification-level diagrams to explore roles.*

153. *Do not use collaboration diagrams to model process flow.*

154. *Create a sequence diagram when sequence is important.*

155. *Apply sequence diagram guidelines to instance-level collaboration diagrams.*

156. *Indicate parameters only when they aren't clear.*

157. *Depict an arrow for each message.*

158. *Consolidate getter invocations.*

159. *Indicate concurrent threads with letters.*

160. *Model "bare" links on instance-level collaboration diagrams.*

161. *Show role-pertinent information on specification-level diagrams.*

162. *Prefer roles on links instead of within classes.*

163. *Indicate navigability sparingly.*

164. *Use links to reflect consistent static relationships.*

UML State Chart Guidelines

165. *Create a state chart when behavior differs based on state.*

166. *Place the initial state in the top-left corner.*

167. *Place the final state in the bottom-right corner.*

168. *State names should be simple but descriptive.*

169. *Question "black-hole" states.*

170. *Question "miracle" states.*

171. *Model substates for targeted complexity.*

172. *Aggregate common substate transitions.*

173. *Create a hierarchy of state charts for very complex entities.*

174. *Always include initial and final states on top-level state charts.*

175. *Name software actions using implementation-language naming conventions.*

176. *Name actor actions using prose.*

177. *Indicate entry actions only when applicable for all entry transitions.*

178. *Indicate exit actions only when applicable for all exit transitions.*

179. *Model recursive transitions only when you want to exit and reenter the state.*

180. *Name transition events in past tense.*

181. *Place transition labels near the source state.*

182. *Place transition labels on the basis of transition direction.*

183. *Do not overlap guards.*

184. *Introduce junctions to visually localize guards.*

185. *Use guards even if they do not form a complete set.*

186. *Never place a guard on an initial transition.*

187. *Use consistent language naming guards.*

UML Activity Diagram Guidelines

188. *Place the start point in the top-left corner.*

189. *Include an ending point.*

190. *Simplify operations requiring flow charts.*

191. *Question "black-hole" activities.*

192. *Question "miracle" activities.*

193. *Reflect the previous activity by using decision points.*

194. *Avoid superfluous decision points.*

195. *Ensure that each transition leaving a decision point has a guard.*

196. *Do not overlap guards.*

197. *Ensure that guards on decision points form a complete set.*

198. *Ensure that exit transition guards and activity invariants form a complete set.*

199. *Apply an [otherwise] guard for "fall-through" logic.*

200. *Model guards only if they add value.*

201. *Ensure that forks have corresponding joins.*

202. *Ensure that a fork has only one entry transition.*

203. *Ensure that a join has only one exit transition.*

204. *Avoid superfluous forks.*

205. *Order swimlanes in a logical manner.*

206. *Apply swimlanes to linear processes.*

207. *Have less than five swimlanes.*

208. *Consider swimareas for complex diagrams.*

209. *Reorganize into smaller activity diagrams when swimareas include several activities.*

210. *Consider horizontal swimlanes for business processes.*

211. *Model the key activities in the primary swimlane.*

212. *Place shared action objects on swimlane separators.*

213. *Apply state names when an object appears several times.*

214. *Reflect the life-cycle stage of an action object in its state name.*

215. *Show only critical inputs and outputs.*

216. *Depict action objects as smaller than activities.*

UML Component Diagram Guidelines

217. *Apply descriptive names to architectural components.*

218. *Apply environment-specific naming conventions to detailed design components.*

219. *Apply consistent textual stereotypes.*

220. *Avoid modeling data and user interface components.*

221. *Prefer lollipop notation to depict interfaces realized by components.*

222. *Prefer the left-hand side of a component for interface lollipops.*

223. *Show only relevant interfaces.*

224. *Model dependencies from left to right.*

225. *Place inheriting components below base components.*

226. *Make components dependent only on interfaces.*

227. *Avoid modeling compilation dependencies.*

UML Deployment Diagram Guidelines

228. *Indicate software components on project-specific diagrams.*

229. *Focus on nodes and communication associations on enterprise-level diagrams.*

230. *Group common nodes.*
231. *Use descriptive terms to name nodes.*
232. *Model only vital software components.*
233. *Apply consistent stereotypes to components.*
234. *Apply visual stereotypes to nodes.*
235. *Indicate communication protocols via stereotypes.*
236. *Model only critical dependencies between components.*

Bibliography

Ambler, S. W. (1997). *Building Object Applications That Work: Your Step-by-Step Handbook for Developing Robust Systems with Object Technology.* New York: Cambridge University Press.
www.ambysoft.com/buildingObjectApplications.html

Ambler, S. W. (1998). *Process Patterns—Building Large-Scale Systems Using Object Technology.* New York: Cambridge University Press.
www.ambysoft.com/processPatterns.html

Ambler, S. W. (2000). *The Enterprise Unified Process (EUP).*
www.ronin-intl.com/publications/unifiedProcess.html

Ambler, S. W. (2001). *The Object Primer, 2nd Edition: The Application Developer's Guide to Object Orientation.* New York: Cambridge University Press.
www.ambysoft.com/theObjectPrimer.html.

Ambler, S. W. (2002). *Agile Modeling: Best Practices for the Unified Process and Extreme Programming.* New York: John Wiley & Sons.
www.ambysoft.com/agileModeling.html.

Beck, K. (2000). *Extreme Programming Explained—Embrace Change.* Reading, MA: Addison-Wesley Longman.

Coad, P., Lefebvre, E., & DeLuca, J. (1999). *Java Modeling in Color with UML: Enterprise Components and Process.* Upper Saddle River, NJ: Prentice-Hall.

Cockburn, A. (2001). *Writing Effective Use Cases.* Boston: Addison-Wesley.

Constantine, L. L., and Lockwood, L. A. D. (1999). *Software for Use: A Practical Guide to the Models and Methods of Usage-Centered Design.* New York: ACM Press.

Douglass, B. P. (1999). *Doing Hard Time: Developing Real-Time Systems with UML, Objects, Frameworks, and Patterns.* Reading, MA: Addison-Wesley Longman.

Evitts, P. (2000). *A UML Pattern Language.* Indianapolis: Macmillan Technical Publishing USA.

Fowler, M. (1999). *Refactoring: Improving the Design of Existing Code.* Menlo Park, CA: Addison-Wesley Longman.

Fowler, M., & Scott, K. (1999). *UML Distilled, Second Edition: A Brief Guide to the Standard Object Modeling Language.* Reading, MA: Addison-Wesley Longman.

Gamma, E., Helm, R., Johnson, R., & Vlissides, J. (1995). *Design Patterns: Elements of Reusable Object-Oriented Software.* Reading, MA: Addison-Wesley.

Gane, C., & Sarson, T. (1979). *Structured Systems Analysis: Tools and Techniques.* Englewood Cliffs, NJ: Prentice-Hall.

Hock, D. W. (2000). *Birth of the Chaordic Age.* San Francisco: Berrett-Koehler Publishers, Inc.

Knoernschild, K. (2002). *Java Design: Objects, UML, and Process.* Boston: Addison-Wesley Longman.

Larman, C. (2002). *Applying UML and Patterns: An Introduction to Object-Oriented Analysis and Design and the Unified Process.* Upper Saddle River, NJ: Prentice-Hall.

Miller, G. A. (1957). The magical number seven, plus or minus two: Some limits on our capacity for processing information. *Psychological Review*, vol. 63, pp. 81–97.
www.well.com/user/smalin/miller.html

Object Management Group (2001). *The Unified Modeling Language (UML) Specification v1.4.*
www.omg.org/technology/documents/formal/uml.htm

Rational Corporation (2002). *Rational Unified Process 2002.*
www.rational.com/products/rup/index.jsp

Riel, A. J. (1996). *Object-Oriented Design Heuristics.* Reading, MA: Addison-Wesley Longman.

Roman, E., Ambler, S. W., & Jewell, T. (2002). *Mastering Enterprise Java Beans, 2/e.* New York: John Wiley & Sons.

Rosenberg, D., & Scott, K. (1999). *Use Case Driven Object Modeling with UML: A Practical Approach.* Reading, MA: Addison-Wesley Longman.

Rumbaugh, J., Jacobson, I., & Booch, G. (1999). *The Unified Modeling Language Reference Manual.* Reading, MA: Addison-Wesley Longman.

Schneider, G., & Winters, J. P. (2001). *Applying Use Cases: A Practical Guide 2/e.* Reading, MA: Addison-Wesley Longman.

Strunk, W., Jr., & White, E. B. (1979). The Elements of Style. New York: Macmillan.

U2 Partners (2002). *The Unified Modeling Language 2.0 Proposal v0.69 (draft).*
cgi.omg.org/docs/ad/02-04-05.pdf

Vermeulen, A., Ambler, S. W., Bumgardner, G., Metz, E., Misfeldt, T., Shur, J., & Thompson, P. (2000). *The Elements of Java Style.* New York: Cambridge University Press.

Warmer, J., & Kleppe, A. (1999). *The Object Constraint Language: Precise Modeling with UML.* Reading, MA: Addison-Wesley Longman.

Index